"Doug Smith is, quite simply, the finest short story writer Canada has ever produced in the science fiction and fantasy genres, and he's also the most prolific. His stories are a treasure trove of riches that will touch your heart while making you think."
—*Robert J. Sawyer, Hugo Award-winning author*

"One of Canada's most original writers of speculative fiction."
— *Library Journal*

"A great storyteller with a gifted and individual voice."
—*Charles de Lint, World Fantasy Award winner*

"Smith's writing, evocative yet understated, gracefully brings to life his imagined realms."
—*Quill and Quire*

"Smith paints his worlds so well that you are transported within a paragraph or two and remain in transit until the story ends."
—*Broken Pencil*

"His stories resonate with a deep understanding of the human condition as well as a characteristic wry wonder... Stories you can't forget, even years later."
—*Julie Czerneda, award-winning author and editor*

"An extraordinary author whom every lover of quality speculative fiction should read."
— *Fantasy Book Critic*

"Smith is definitely an author who deserves to be more widely read."
—*Strange Horizons*

"Sadly under read, Douglas Smith is deserving of an entire 'Science Fiction You Haven't Read...But Should' article all to his own, and you'll likely see it one day."
—*Digital Science Fiction*

PLAYING THE SHORT GAME:

How to Market and Sell Short Fiction

By Douglas Smith

Lucky Bat Books

A Lucky Bat Book

Playing The Short Game:
How to Market and Sell Short Fiction

Cover Art & Design by Erik Mohr

Published by Lucky Bat Books

LuckyBatBooks.com

10 9 8 7 6 5 4 3 2 1

ISBN: 978-1-928048-22-0

Also available in ebook (ISBN: 978-1-928048-23-7)

Discover other titles by the author at

www.smithwriter.com

CONTENTS

INTRODUCTION

BY KRISTINE KATHRYN RUSCH

NOVELISTS THINK OF short stories as afterthoughts. Oh, they tell each other, you can always write a short story.

They say that with a bit of a snobbish air, as if short stories are beneath them. They sit on their lofty 100,000 word perches and sneer at the writers who toil in the short fiction arena as if those writers really aren't worthy.

Until the novels-only novelists try to write a short story, and realize just how hard it is. They can't natter on for pages about how someone looks or reveal that he grew up with a German Shepherd, unless that dog is part of the short story's plot.

For a while in the 1980s and 1990s, it looked like the short story might die of neglect. Only a few markets still published them in the genres. Outside of the genres, the literary press cut back on the short stories that it published as well—at least the stories that it paid for. If a short story writer wanted to sell something for copies of the publication, well, there were hundreds of those "markets."

I put the word in quotes because, as a professional writer, I don't give my work away, and the places that ask me to, saying I'll get prestige, apparently don't realize that I can't eat prestige.

About ten years ago now, it became possible again to make a living selling just short fiction. A short fiction writer would have to write a lot of short fiction each year, and would have to be very good at marketing it, but the writer could make about a hefty five-figure income.

It took concentration; it meant the writer had to know her markets. It meant she had to understand contracts, and she had to look outside of her native land for reprint sales. But it could be done.

I know, because I did it.

I also sold novels at the time, but the short fiction made as much as four novel sales each and every year.

Fortunately for me, I love short stories, and I love writing them. I've edited them, I've written them, and I've owned publishing companies dedicated to publishing them. I blog about them even now, and I subscribe to almost every genre short fiction magazine I can get my hands on.

The short fiction market has greatly improved since the publishing industry started to change about five years ago. The rise of electronic publishing saved some of the genre magazines, and inspired others to start. Suddenly, the magazines could get worldwide subscribers with just a click of a button. A reader overseas didn't have to pay massive shipping costs to read something curated by their favorite editor.

At least once a quarter, I donate to some Kickstarter project dedicated to funding a new magazine. At least once a quarter, I also donate to other Kickstarters funding a new anthology. Heck, I'm even back editing, and I said I wouldn't do that unless I had complete creative control, something I didn't have at The Magazine of Fantasy & Science Fiction, back in the 1990s when I edited the magazine.

The short fiction markets haven't just grown: They've exploded.

And not just in science fiction or mystery. Literary journals are actually paying money again. Romance anthologies have received major funding.

I suspect that writers could probably make more than the median income in the United States with short stories alone, as long as they keep their heads down and write a lot of short work.

Writing short takes skill. It takes craft and a dedication that novel-only writers don't quite understand. New ideas weekly, a willingness to venture into creatively unknown territory, and on and on and on. The craft side alone of writing short fiction could take up an entire volume—and has.

(Ignore those books that tell you to spend a year or more on your short story; That's for amateurs. If you want to be a professional writer—and why would you buy this book if you didn't?—then write and mail a short story per week for one year. Just try it. What can it hurt?)

No one, to my knowledge, has written an entire book on the business of short fiction.

Until now.

Douglas Smith is the best person to write this book. Sure, Library Journal called him "One of Canada's most original writers of speculative fiction" and the marvelous Charles de Lint praised him. Doug has won or been nominated for dozens of awards, not just in Canada, but in France and the United States as well.

He's one of the few people who has probably published more short fiction than I have, and in more countries, and more high-paying markets. He loves the short story as much as I do, and he's good at writing them.

He's just as good at the business side of the profession. He knows more about marketing short stories to other countries than I do. He understands how to manage short fiction contracts very well. He's up-to-date on 21st century publishing practices, and he has a toughness that the best business people need.

We short story writers have needed a book like this for decades.

I'm glad Doug decided to write it.

Read and reread this volume. Because you'll learn something each time you do. And take Doug's advice. It's spectacular.

Don't take my word for it.

Turn the page and dive in.

By the time you're done, I'll wager you'll be recommending this book to your writer friends—just like I have.

—Kristine Kathryn Rusch
Lincoln City, Oregon
April 30, 2014

ABOUT THIS BOOK
(AND HOW TO USE IT)

HI AND WELCOME! Congratulations, too! By buying this book, you've taken your first step towards selling more stories and building a career as a professional short fiction writer.

Who This Book Is For

I wrote this book for the beginning short fiction writer who wants to learn how best to market and sell their stories. More experienced writers will also find value in these pages, but my target audience is the beginning writer.

Also, although many of my examples in this book relate to genre short fiction—science fiction (SF), fantasy, mystery, horror (since that's what I write myself)—the advice I give applies to *all and any short fiction writing*.

Who I Am and Why I Can Help You

I've been selling short stories since 1997 and selling them regularly with multiple sales each year. I have over a hundred and fifty short fiction publications in thirty countries and twenty-five languages around the world, including top professional markets such as *Amazing Stories*, *InterZone*, *Cicada*, *Baen's Universe*, *Weird Tales*, and *The Mammoth Book of Best New Horror*.

I have three collections of short fiction: *Chimerascope* (ChiZine, 2010), *Impossibilia* (PS Publishing, 2008), and a translated fantasy collection, *La Danse des Esprits* (Dreampress, France, 2011).

I've won Canada's Aurora Award for short fiction three times and have been a finalist another sixteen times. I was a finalist for the international John W. Campbell Award for best new writer. My collections have been finalists for Canada's juried Sunburst Award, the

Canadian Broadcasting Corporation's Bookies Award, and France's juried Prix Masterton and Prix Bob Morane.

One of my short stories was made into a short film, and I've also published a novel, *The Wolf at the End of the World*. Check out my website at www.smithwriter.com for more information on my writing.

And if you are still not convinced, here's a quote from Hugo and Nebula award-winning author, Robert J. Sawyer:

"Douglas Smith is, quite simply, the finest short story writer Canada has ever produced in the science fiction and fantasy genres, and he's also the most prolific. His stories are a treasure trove of riches that will touch your heart while making you think."

But in the end, you will decide if my advice in this book is worthwhile based on its value to you. So let's get started.

What This Book Will Cover

In Section One, we set a foundation for the rest of the book and your short fiction career. I ask you to consider why you are writing and what kind of writer you are at this point in your career. I ask you to consider the career you want as a writer and what you are willing to invest to achieve your dream. We then review the many benefits of writing short fiction for any writer planning a long-term career. Finally, we look at why you never actually "sell" a story and learn about licensing rights for short fiction.

With this critical foundation in place, you will be ready for the next two sections, which mirror the steps a story goes through from its initial marketing to its sale, and then through the publishing process to its final publication.

Section Two covers everything you must understand about marketing and selling a story. We start with learning to know when your story is ready to send out. Next, we cover finding markets and how to select the right *first* market for your story. We'll discuss how to submit stories, how to handle rejections, and what to do with stories that keep being rejected. You'll also learn how editors decide on what stories they choose to purchase and what ones they reject.

In Section Three, we begin the happier topic of what happens when you sell a story. Here, we'll cover short fiction contracts, working with editors, dealing with reviews, and what to expect after you sell your first story.

In Section Four, we move into topics of relevance to writers who have begun to sell regularly and are building their backlist—their inventory of sold stories. Here we talk about leveraging the rights to your fiction, including selling reprints, selling translations, and publishing collections. We close off this section with a look at indie publishing options for short fiction writers.

Finally, in Section Five, we consider the longer term aspects of a short fiction career once a writer has multiple story sales to their credit, and how you can leverage your short fiction into a novel writing career.

Check out the Table of Contents for a detailed list of the topics we'll cover in each of these sections.

What This Book Will Not Cover

I will *not* be dealing with the *creative* side of writing fiction. I won't tell you how to write a story or how to improve your craft. We start from the point where you have at least one short story finished and ready to send out into the cold, cruel world.

Why not start with the craft side? Well, for one thing, teaching the craft of fiction is harder. Selling short fiction is straightforward. All it takes is a basic knowledge of how things work, a thick skin, and stubborn persistence. Once you understand the process, you'll realize it's a numbers game—a game won by the writer who keeps the most stories out in front of the most markets. Seriously, that's the secret. I'll repeat that advice throughout this book, and I hope that once you learn how short fiction markets work, you'll understand why that advice is so true.

But trying to teach someone how to *write* short fiction is another story, no pun intended. Writing is a very personal process for every writer. What works for me may not work for you. And you may not write the same kind of stories I do. My creative writing advice would start from the way I write, which begins with character and point of view. Another writer might start with the idea or the plot or the world. Yes, you need all those elements for a good story, but every writer takes a different route to get to where they type "The End."

How to Use This Book

As mentioned above, the sequence of this book mirrors the steps a new writer needs to follow when they begin to send their stories out into the world and then start to sell those stories. So the short answer to "How to Use This Book" is to read it *in order*.

Further, if you can, take one of your stories and use it to follow along in the process, especially for the steps in Section Two where you learn how to market your stories. Pick a story. Decide if it is ready to market. Use the resources and advice in this book to find markets for that story. Decide which markets to send it to first. Write a cover letter for that story and send it to that market.

And when you sell that story (and you will), follow the sequence in section Three to review the contract and to work with the editor to get your great tale published.

In other words, I wrote this book in a specific order for a reason, with each chapter building on knowledge and advice laid out in the prior ones. So treat the book as if it were a course you're taking—and don't skip any lectures.

Once you've sold a few stories, use the book as a reference to refresh your memory or deal with a situation you haven't encountered before, whether that be understanding rights and contract terms or putting together a collection.

So please, start at Chapter One and follow along as we learn how to take a story from submission to sale to publication...and beyond. And in that process, you will learn how to build your reputation and career as a short fiction writer.

Ready? Let's begin!

SECTION I

SETTING A FOUNDATION:

THE FUNDAMENTALS

To BEGIN OUR journey, we need to set a strong foundation of knowledge for you as a short fiction writer, along with a few key expectations.

In this section, I ask you to consider the type of writer you are at this point in your career and to reflect on whether you need an attitude adjustment. I also ask you to think about why you're writing and the type of career you want to have as a writer. Most importantly, I ask you to seriously consider how much you are willing to invest to achieve your dream.

We then look at the many benefits of writing short fiction for any writer, whether you are planning a career in short fiction or novels.

Finally, we learn why you never "sell" a story, as we discuss the licensing of rights for short fiction, essential knowledge for every writer.

CHAPTER 1.
WHY ARE YOU WRITING?:
Deciding on the Writing Career You Want

BEFORE WE START this journey, I want you to think about *why* you want to be a writer and what *kind* of writer you want to be. What will success look like for you? What are your goals?

In short, what is your writing dream?

If you're a beginning writer, you might immediately respond that you just want to sell your first story. I get that. When you're starting out, it's hard to imagine how far you might be able to go. Just getting your first sale feels like scaling Everest, doesn't it?

But for now, put aside any fears or doubts you have on whether you *can* reach your dream. Right now, think of what you'll do *after* your first sale (after taking time to bask in the warm glow).

Is that it? Will that be enough for you? Or will you want to sell another story? And another? Do you plan to move on to novels eventually? Are you already writing novels? Do you dream of a career as a full-time fiction writer?

Most importantly (because it's easy to simply say you want to be the next J. K. Rowling or Stephen King), ask yourself whether you're willing to pay the *price* for your dream.

That price is hard work. Work devoted to learning your craft. Work devoted to writing new words, then revising those words, and then writing still more new words. In short, work devoted to learning *how* to be a writer. And that means a *lot* of time as well as effort—time *not* doing other things in your life.

Before you decide on your answer, let's look at the two most common types of beginning writers.

The Arrogant Beginner

The first kind doesn't accept that they're a beginner. They've written a few stories or their first novel, and they can't understand why editors keep rejecting their work. Maybe their stories haven't found the right market yet, but for this type of beginner, it's likely because their stories simply aren't very good.

And that's okay. After all, they're a beginner at the *craft* of writing. Beginners will always suffer when compared to professionals who've done that craft for years. And when you try to sell your work, whether as a beginner or an established writer, you will always be competing against the best of the professionals.

But these arrogant new writers don't understand they're beginners. They won't accept they need to learn their craft, so they never do the work required to develop their writing. Confidence is a good thing. Arrogance combined with ignorance—not so much.

Since I'm Canadian, let me indulge in a hockey metaphor. Expecting to write at the professional level in your early attempts is like expecting you'll play like Wayne Gretzky or Sydney Crosby the first time you strap on skates. Guess what? You won't. You'll fall flat on your face.

And that's okay, too—as long as you get up each time and keep trying. And "keep trying" does *not* mean sending out the same crappy story over and over. Later, I *will* tell you to keep submitting your stories, but then I will assume you've done the work to learn your craft.

"Keep trying" means being willing to do what Gretzky, Crosby, and every other human who dominated their chosen profession did. They put in long hours of practice, practice, and more practice to continually learn their craft and hone their skills. In short, keep getting up when you fall. Keep practising to be better, to learn how not to fall, and (eventually) to learn how to excel.

So if you won't accept that you're a beginner, that you have much to learn, and that you need to devote time and effort to learn your craft as a writer, just stop right now. Or at least quit whining about rejections (and get used to them).

The Fearful Beginner

The second kind of beginner is a mirror image of the first. They don't think anything they write is ever good enough. They are constantly rewriting the same story or finishing stories but never sending them out, or not sending them to the top markets when they do. Ironically, these writers often *are* putting in the time and effort to learn their craft. Their early stories are generally better than those of the arrogant, lazy beginners mentioned above.

The problem with this type of beginner isn't arrogance or laziness—it's fear.

If you're reading this book, you already have some kind of writing dream. So here's the thing about a dream—as long as you never chase it, you can never fail. That dream will always exist in your head, perfect and immaculate, with the eternal possibility it will come true. Of course, if you never chase that dream, there it will always remain: in your head—unrealized, unfulfilled, a possible wonderful life for you that will *never* come true.

Fear enters this because if you *do* chase a dream, you introduce the possibility of failure. You fear you'll discover you can't reach your dream. And then, the beginner thinks, their dream will die. And that is scary. I believe it's the main reason most people never achieve their dreams. They don't even try—because they're afraid to fail.

If you see yourself in this description of the fearful beginner, do me a favor...no, do *yourself* a favor.

7

Just try. Try to follow your dream.

Trust me in this—if you're willing to do the work to learn and practice your craft, you will eventually produce stories of a professional quality. And if you're stubborn and persistent, develop a thick skin about rejections, and follow the advice in this book, you will sell those stories.

Some of you will reach that point sooner than others, but as long as you don't quit, you *will* sell what you write.

Balancing Confidence and Caution

The key for developing as a writer is to narrow the spectrum in which you operate. You need to learn to range between confidence (not arrogance) and caution (not fear), depending on the writing activity.

When you're writing first drafts, you need to be confident. But when you finish that draft, you need to slide over to caution, recognizing that your work isn't perfect and needs editing and review.

When you're sending your work out to markets and dealing with rejections, confidence must rule you again. As you will learn, you need to keep your stories in the mail until they sell.

But when you sell that story, caution should take over again as you review the contract to understand what you're signing. And when you're working with the editor on changes to your story, you should be wary of any arrogance that tempts you to push back on suggestions that will make your story stronger.

Don't worry if you don't understand some of the above situations yet. We'll be covering all of these in the course of this book.

So right now, humor me. If you see yourself in either the arrogant or the fearful beginner, decide how you'll change. Accept that you're a beginner and put in the time to learn your craft. Put aside your fears and let yourself try to reach your dream of a writing career, whatever kind of dream that might be.

The Dream and the Price

Now I need you to think about that dream. Why? Pretend this is a car dealership you just walked into, and I'm the salesperson. Before you listen to advice I give about what kind of car you should buy, you need to know what you're looking for. A basic get-me-to-the-train-station, no-frills runabout (you want to sell one story to prove you can do it, and then will probably never write again)? Or the top-of-the-line, all-the-bells-and-whistles, luxury car (full-time professional career)?

You also need to decide how much you're willing to spend. Are you on a very tight budget (not willing to do much work or spend much time)? Or is the price no object (will write and practice regularly until you reach your dream)?

Ironically, these two points (what you aiming for and what you're willing to spend) are typically out of synch in my two types of beginners. The Arrogant Beginner wants to be J. K. Rowling but isn't willing to do the work. The Fearful Beginner is often already paying the price by doing the work, but is dreaming too small.

What I'm Selling

Now that you've thought about your dream writing career, I'm going to tell you what sort of dealership you've walked into.

Sorry, but I'm only selling luxury cars here. My advice is aimed at beginners who want to be professional writers. I'll show you how to make the most from each story you write, how to sell your stories to the best market you can find, and how to make your short fiction work for you for more exposure and revenue sources. In short, how to build a short fiction career as a base for a full-time writing career.

If that isn't your writing dream, you will still get value from this book. You just may apply my advice differently or decide some options really aren't for you. But if you decide against a professional career, I hope it's because you don't want to invest the time and effort, rather than not believing you can do it.

Because you can — if you want it enough.

CHAPTER 2.
WHY SHORT FICTION?:
Its Benefits to a Writing Career

I LOVE SHORT stories, both to read and to write. You may or may not agree. If you're in the latter group, don't worry. I'm not suggesting you write only short fiction. If you're writing novels now, keep doing so. But I am recommending that even novelists should include short fiction in their writing career plan. I'm still following that same advice myself—although I'm focusing on novels now, I continue to write and publish short stories.

When I began writing, I intentionally started with short stories for three reasons: to learn how to write fiction, to discover if I could sell what I wrote, and to build my credentials. All good reasons, but short fiction has other benefits for beginners as well. Let's look at them all.

Learn Your Craft

First, and most importantly, writing short stories is an excellent way to learn the *craft* of fiction. Short stories let you learn to use many of the key tools you need in your writer's toolbox, whether you write short stories or novels. Those tools include: handling point of view (POV), story and scene structure, characterization, plot, pacing, special scenes (beginnings, flashbacks, endings, denouement, etc.), dialog, setting description, world building, exposition, information flow, linking symbolism, voice, and genre, not to mention basic sentence structure, paragraphing, punctuation, grammar, and syntax.

Yes, if you move to novels, you'll find still more skills to learn, such as more complex plotting, sub-plots, deeper character development, handling a larger cast of characters, bigger ideas, and pacing (again), just to mention a few. But at least you'll start with a level of proficiency in many of the key skills you'll need for longer works.

Short stories also offer a unique advantage over novels in learning your craft, because they're...well, short. They let you experiment with different techniques and approaches from one story to another, practising a different tool with each story.

Perhaps all your stories so far have used limited third-person POV in past tense, and you want to try writing in first-person, present tense. Or try a story with an unreliable narrator or an unsympathetic main character. Or a story where the POV character is not the main character. Or a story heavy on dialog or setting description. Or you've been writing science fiction, and you want to try fantasy or horror or mystery.

Or whatever. The point is you can develop more techniques and practise more aspects of your writing in twenty 5,000-word short stories than you can in one 100,000-word novel.

Test the Waters

When I started, I had no idea whether I'd ever be able to sell anything I wrote. So I decided I'd rather invest the time in writing and trying to sell short stories than in writing and marketing a novel. It just seemed a smaller hill to climb to find out if I could sell my fiction.

That reasoning will probably appeal to the Fearful Beginner we met in Chapter One. It's amazing what an encouraging rejection on a story, not to mention that first sale, can do to your confidence. Short fiction provides you an opportunity to get feedback on the progress of your craft much earlier than does the novel route. More on that in Section Two.

Build Your Resume

For many years, especially in genre fiction, the experts advised new writers that short fiction was the best way to "break in" and build a reputation with sales and awards.

It's no longer the obvious way to start, but the argument still holds great value. Once you can include sales to *professional* markets (note the emphasis) in your cover letters, you'll start to climb out of the slush piles. More on this benefit when we cover slush piles and the selection process editors follow in Section Two.

A story in a professional market also brings the chance of getting on award ballots and maybe even winning, as well as of being selected for one of the several annual "Best of" anthologies. We'll discuss these more in Section Five.

Generate or Explore Ideas for Novels

On the creative side, short fiction provides the opportunity to generate bigger ideas and take them for a test drive. You may discover as you write a story that this particular idea is bigger than you first imagined. Or you really enjoy these characters. Or find they have a larger tale to tell, a tale that requires a novel. Short stories also let you explore an existing idea for a novel, or to play around in that universe a bit before tackling it in longer form.

The first story I wrote (and sold), "Spirit Dance," led to more stories and a novel in the same universe. I wrote "Memories of the Dead Man" to explore the title character from the points of view of other characters before writing a novel in his world.

Build a Backlist

As you write and sell short fiction, you'll build your *backlist*: your inventory of published stories for which you retain the rights or for which the rights have reverted to you. That assumes, of course, you didn't give those rights away by signing a bad contract.

We'll cover licensing of rights in Chapter Three and short fiction contracts in Chapter Fourteen. For now, understand that if you handle the rights to your fiction correctly, you will have a backlist you can "sell" again and again (you'll understand the quotes after the next chapter). This includes reprints of your stories, foreign language translations, collections of your short fiction, and independently publishing your backlist. We'll talk more about leveraging your backlist in Section Four.

Build a Network

As you begin to make contact with editors and as you sell your stories, you will also start to build your network in the writing world. This will take time, but if you're reasonable to work with and meet your deadlines, editors will ask you to submit to invitation-only anthologies or special magazine issues. Or they might propose publishing a collection of your work. All of those events have happened to me multiple times.

Learn the Publishing Business (Sort of)

Short fiction also gives you exposure to and experience with one portion of the publishing industry. Now, short story publishing is hugely different from novel publishing, especially in the marketing process, the markets you'll deal with, and the legal and contractual complexities you'll encounter.

But just as many aspects of short story craft help in writing novels, so are there aspects of short fiction *publishing* that will help when you move to novels. These include knowing when your work is ready for market, finding markets, understanding licensing and rights, dealing with rejections, dealing with editors, understanding basic contract terms, dealing with editing and copy-editing requests, and the administration of tracking of submissions, publications, contributor copies, and, of course, getting paid.

Money (Sort of)

The minimum professional rate in speculative fiction markets is six cents a word right now, or just $300 for a first rights sale of a 5,000-word short story. Some markets pay more. Most pay much less, but you won't be submitting to those, as we'll discuss in Section Two.

So you won't get rich. But if you write fast and well and in multiple genres, and if you retain and leverage the multiple rights for your stories, you can certainly supplement your income. Just don't plan to quit your day job. We'll look at generating multiple income streams from your fiction in depth in Section Four.

So by now, I hope you're convinced that, regardless of the writing career you're planning, including short fiction as part of your plan just makes good sense.

CHAPTER 3.
WHY YOU NEVER "SELL" A STORY:
Rights and Licensing

THIS IS THE most important chapter in this book. Here, we cover one of the most critical topics for a writer to understand if they want a professional career: the licensing of rights for fiction.

A Caveat: Do Your Homework

This is *not* an exhaustive discussion on rights and licensing. We'll cover only the basics, just enough for you to understand the key elements and hopefully realize how very important this topic is to your writing career.

First, a caveat. I'll steal a favorite quote from a writing mentor of mine, the multi-award winning, multi-genre writer, Kristine Kathryn Rusch. Kris likes to preface any quasi-legal advice she gives with "I am not a lawyer nor do I play one on TV."

In other words, you need to do your *own* research on this topic and do it early in your career. If in doubt when dealing with a rights situation in your career, get advice from a professional writer or an intellectual property lawyer. Having said that, for short fiction contracts, which we cover in Chapter Fourteen, I have never needed a lawyer (novel contracts are a different matter).

To better understand rights and licensing, I recommend you buy "The Copyright Handbook" (Nolo Press). It's updated every year, so don't buy it used. It will take you a few passes to get through, but if you're planning a writing career, it will be time well spent.

While I'm mentioning Kris Rusch, I'll strongly recommend her weekly blog, "The Business Rusch" (http://kriswrites.com/business-rusch-publishing-articles/), as well as Dean Wesley Smith's two blog series, "Think Like a Publisher" (http://www.deanwesleysmith.com/?page_id=3736) and "Killing the Sacred Cows of Publishing" (http://www.deanwesleysmith.com/?page_id=860).

So with the above caveats in mind, let's start.

Copyright and Licensing

First, you need to understand you'll never actually "sell" a story. I am not predicting your likelihood of success in a writing career. I mean when your first "sale" occurs, you will not be *selling* anything. Rather, you'll be *licensing* a very particular set of *rights* connected to that story to another party in the person of a publisher.

(A comment on copyright: when you write your story, its copyright is automatically protected. You don't need to register your copyright—that is, file with your particular government—to protect it. A recommended exception: if you're sending anything to Hollywood, you should formally register copyright. You're still protected if you don't, but it will make proving your copyright easier in any subsequent lawsuit should a theft of copyright occur, something which is much more prevalent in Hollywood).

Note that the *idea* in your story is *not* protected by copyright. Copyright protects the *manuscript*: the *form* of the story—the sentence structure, how the words appear. In the US, copyright remains in place for seventy years after your death. If you want to protect it beyond that, check out Kris Rusch's posts on estate planning for writers. There are exceptions to copyright law (the most common that applies to writers is "fair use") but those exceptions are beyond the scope of this book.

The Many Dimensions of Rights

Okay, so you've written a story. You first need to understand you hold multiple rights on the story, rights which you may license (or choose not to) for money (or not) to a third party. These rights have several dimensions:

- Media;
- Language;
- Geography;
- Occurrence; and,
- Time.

These separate dimensions combine with each other to form the particular set of rights you'll license for any story "sale." Let's look at each dimension in turn.

Media Rights

I'm using *media* to refer to the *format or form* in which your story appears and is delivered to the end consumer. The media rights requests you will encounter relate directly to the most common methods of presenting your words in the various short fiction markets today:

- Print rights: the right to reproduce your story in some *physically* (versus electronically) printed form;
- Electronic rights: the right to reproduce your story as an ebook or via an online web page; and,
- Audio rights: the right to reproduce your story as a spoken vocal recording, distributed either as a sound file or accessible via a website link.

For each of those formats, two common types of short fiction markets exist:

- A *magazine* is any publication with a recurring publishing schedule, issue numbers, and usually an International Standard Serial Number or ISSN (versus an ISBN for a book). When you license rights to a magazine, you are selling *serial* rights since these are serial publications.

- An *anthology* is a book-length work containing short stories from *different* authors. (An important note for beginners—do not confuse an anthology with a *collection*, a book-length work of short stories from a *single* author. The two terms are *not* interchangeable.) You license anthology rights to an anthology (duh).

So, for example, you might be selling your story to a print magazine (licensing serial print rights) or an audio anthology (licensing audio anthology rights), or a magazine or anthology which publishes both print and ebook editions (licensing print and electronic rights).

While we're discussing media rights, it's worth mentioning *archival rights* as well. These provide a market with the right to maintain your story in some form of online archive indefinitely after the issue or anthology in which it first appeared is published. Archival rights are associated only with electronic and audio rights and are commonly requested along with those rights.

I'm also using "media" to refer to other formats your story, your story world, or its characters could be presented in or adapted to, beyond the straight-forward publication of your words as you've written them. These other formats include film, games, comics, graphic novels, products (think Star Wars action figures and Spiderman pajamas), and more.

The key point for you to understand as a writer is that *each* of these media formats has *separate* rights associated with it. The possible combinations of rights are limited only by your imagination—or that of a marketing department.

Language Rights

Language rights are easy to understand, but are too often given away by beginners. Most short fiction markets will require rights in only one language, the language in which they publish. To start, beginning writers should only be submitting to English language markets (we'll discuss selling to foreign language markets in detail in Chapter Twenty-One). Certain top professional English magazines legitimately ask for non-English rights as well, as they have standing agreements allowing select foreign magazines to translate any story that appears in the English professional market.

Occurrence Rights

These relate to whether you are licensing *first rights* or *second rights*. You can sell *first* rights for a particular media and language only once—the very first time you sell your story.

Any subsequent time you sell that story, you'll be licensing *second* rights, commonly referred to as selling the story as a reprint. As you'll learn, most professional markets, and certainly the top ones, do not accept reprints *as submissions*. They may publish reprints, but those will typically be classic stories or stories from big name authors. From your perspective, as a beginner or a no-name author, these markets will only purchase first rights.

Note that *any* subsequent sale of a story after you've sold first rights involves licensing *second* rights—not third, fourth, or fifth rights.

Critical for you to understand is that *first and second rights apply to a specific media and language*. For example, you could license first print rights in English for a story to an English print anthology publisher, and still be able to license first audio rights in English for that same story to an audio book publisher, or first print rights in French to a French publisher.

Geographic Rights

Another easy one to understand, and one that is becoming simpler, as electronic editions (ebook, web, audio) of anthologies and magazines become more common for most short fiction markets.

Before the growth of electronic markets, you would typically be licensing geographically constrained rights. For example, a print magazine that physically distributed only in Canada would ask for First Canadian Serial Rights in English. A US magazine might have asked for First North American Serial Rights in English, as they typically distributed in Canada as well as the US. An English language anthology with plans to sell overseas would have asked for World Anthology Rights in English.

Today, any market which includes an electronic version of their publication will ask for Electronic Rights and World Rights in their particular language. Note that if a market asks for World Serial Rights or World Anthology Rights *without* specifying any language, they are asking for *all* languages.

The Time Dimension: Reversion of Rights

Finally, and perhaps most importantly, the rights you license have (or should have) an explicit time period. After such a period has elapsed, the rights you licensed to the short fiction market which published your story *revert to you*. That is, those rights become yours again (except for first rights—you only get to sell those once).

Yes, the rights to your story come back to you—unless you were dumb enough to sign away all of your rights and not include a *rights reversion clause* in your contract. More on this in Chapter Fourteen on contracts. For now just know that if your contract doesn't explicitly state when the rights revert to you, you need to add such a clause.

Typically, for a magazine contract, rights revert to you based on the magazine's publication schedule, usually when the next issue is published. That is, the issue after the one in which your story appeared. So if a magazine publishes every three months, your rights might not revert to you until four to six months after they've published the issue with your story. This is only fair—they don't want you selling your story as a reprint (second rights) and have it appear in a competing market before they've had a chance to sell their issue containing your little tale.

For anthologies, a one-year post-publication reversion clause is common. Again, this longer period is only fair, as book distribution has a longer ramp-up period and needs more time for a publisher to recoup their investment, compared to magazines, which have an existing subscriber base.

Moral Rights

Copyright law protects the *moral rights* of the author. Moral rights give the author the right to protect their work from any use that could potentially harm the author's reputation.

If a publisher requests moral rights, understand that you would be granting that publisher the right, at *their* discretion (not yours) to associate your work or your name with something with which you might not want to be associated.

In the past, you were generally *not* asked to license moral rights to your fiction. However, in recent years, it has become more common, especially for US and British publishers, to demand moral rights in situations where they are buying World English language rights (see above), which again has become the norm.

Under most non-US international copyright law, moral rights are *personal to the author and remain with the author* regardless of what other rights are licensed *unless the author explicitly waives their moral rights*. If waived, the period of the moral rights transfer is the same as the period of the other rights licensed.

Moral rights are dealt with much differently under international copyright law versus U.S. copyright law. The Canadian Copyright Act defines moral rights as including the following (taken from http://en.wikipedia.org/wiki/Moral_rights_in_Canadian_copyright_law):

Right of Paternity: Includes the right to claim authorship, the right to remain anonymous, or the right to use a pseudonym or pen name.

Right of Integrity: In the case of a work being adapted, modified or translated, the author/creator's right of integrity must be respected. … [An] author/creator's right to the integrity of his work is violated if the work is a distortion, mutilation or modification of the work that is prejudicial to the honor or reputation of the author/creator.

Right of Association: … [An] author/creator has the right to prevent anyone from using his work in association with a product, service, cause, or institution.

Copyright law in the U.S. allows moral rights to be transferred along with copyright. Apparently to comply with international copyright treaties, the U.S. added moral rights to their Copyright Act, but the definition of moral rights used is not as inclusive as above. In the U.S., moral rights give the author the right to:

- Claim authorship for a work;
- Prevent the use of the author's name on any work not created by the author;
- Prevent intentional distortion or mutilation that prejudices the author's honor or reputation; and,
- Prevent the destruction of famous works.

(from depts.washington.edu/uwcopy/Copyright_Law/International_Copyright_Law/Differences.php)

Personally, if a market asks for moral rights, I will *not* sign the contract. But again, folks, I am not a lawyer, so do your own research before signing any contract. Your career, your decision.

A Special Situation: Work-for-Hire

In work-for-hire situations, you are a contracted writer employed by a corporation. In most cases, you give up *all rights* to any work you produce under a work-for-hire contract. The corporation owns anything you produce as their contractor. Typical work-for-hire situations include writing tie-in novels to any major media product, such as anything in the Marvel, Star Trek, or Star Wars universes. It's analogous to being an employee with a company, where anything you produce during your employment is legally the intellectual property of your employer.

Work-for-hire contracts generally pay well, but on a one-time, flat fee basis. You're giving up any future earnings potential from reselling your work down the road. Legally, it's not your work—all rights for the work are owned entirely by whoever hired you.

Examples of Licensing Rights to Short Fiction

Let's look at a few possible examples of what rights you could reasonably expect to be asked to license for common types of short fiction sales. Note that these examples are for "first rights" sales—that is, non-reprints:

- A print magazine in the US that does not take reprints and has no ebook edition and no distribution outside North America will require First North American Serial Rights in English;

- The same magazine but with additional distribution in the UK will require First World Serial Rights in English. Yes, they might ask for just UK and NA rights, but if they're selling outside the US, they're probably selling to other English markets, too, or plan to;

- If the same magazine offers an ebook version of each issue, they will also require First Electronic Serial Rights (you can and should specifically exclude audio rights from the definition of "electronic");

- An anthology that plans to publish both print and ebook editions in English will require First World Anthology Rights in English and First Electronic Rights in English. If they plan to sell foreign rights to the anthology, they will ask for First World Anthology and First Electronic Rights (no language specified).

- A web-only magazine will require First Electronic Rights (world rights are implied) in English. Note that if they don't take reprints, they will expect you *not* to have previously sold first *print* rights either. That same web-only magazine will also likely request Archival Rights.

- A podcast or audio magazine will require First Audio Rights in English. Note that most (but not all) audio magazines and anthologies will not care if the story has appeared before in text format (print or electronic). In fact, many of the top audio markets prefer stories that have already been published in text. More on audio markets in Chapter Twenty-Two.

Judging a Request for Rights: Is It Necessary? Is the Price Fair?

In the above examples, I used the term "require," meaning these are the *minimum* set of rights the market must license from you to legally publish the particular magazine or anthology in the formats and geographies specified.

That doesn't mean they won't ask for *additional* rights. It's up to you to not license rights to them they don't need, rights you could sell separately to another market. For example, it's becoming more common for a market to ask for electronic and audio rights even if they only currently publish a print edition. These are "just in case" rights grabs, and you should request their removal from your contract.

Another common rights request in short fiction magazine contracts is for anthology rights along with serial rights, for situations where the magazine publishes an annual or periodic "Best of" anthology containing stories selected from their prior issues. Sometimes the magazine will offer an additional fee for these rights, sometimes not. You'll need to decide if you're okay with such a request. For me, if it's a major market paying professional rates, I'm usually happy to leave that clause in and have a chance to get additional visibility by appearing in the anthology.

The contract will typically identify these additional anthology rights as "non-exclusive" since they are second (reprint) rights, meaning you can license those rights again. Yes, that's right—you can sell reprints of a story as many times as you're able to find markets willing to buy them. More on that in Chapter Twenty.

For the beginner, the issue of rights can be confusing, especially when a market is asking for more rights than you expected. You'll learn with experience, but a good test to apply is whether you feel a rights request is both *necessary* and *fair*.

First, are these rights *necessary* for the market to publish your story in their present form? If they currently only publish in English, for example, why are they asking for all language rights?

Second, is the *price* they're offering fair for any requested additional rights? If they're a magazine requesting anthology rights because they might publish an annual "Best of" anthology, are they offering *additional fees at a professional rate* for your story should that anthology be published? Are they a major magazine paying top professional rates? If so, you might be comfortable in licensing those additional rights.

Your Career, Your Responsibility

We'll cover more on licensing rights, including how to say no to unfair rights requests, when we discuss short fiction contracts in Chapter Fourteen. For now, you should have enough knowledge to be able to read the submission guidelines for short fiction markets more critically to understand which rights the market will need if they buy your story.

Again, what we've covered here is a *very* high-level overview. Remember my quote from Kris Rusch: "I'm not a lawyer nor do I play one on TV." It's *your* responsibility to understand the licensing of rights for your fiction.

If you're a beginner, you probably won't believe me, but I repeat: this chapter is the most important one in this book. Reread and study it until you understand it thoroughly. Then, do your own research and learn about rights and licensing.

Because in the end, it's your story, your decision, and your career.

SECTION II

SELLING SHORT:

HOW TO MARKET
YOUR STORIES

WITH THE CRITICAL foundation from Section One now in place, you are ready to learn about marketing and selling your short fiction.

We'll focus on selling first rights to a story. We'll start with how to decide when your story is ready to send to a market. Next, we'll look at how to find markets, how to select the right ones, and how to select where to submit first.

Next, we'll cover how to submit stories (and how not to), how to deal with rejections, and what to do with stories that keep getting rejected. We'll also look at how editors make decisions on what stories they reject and what ones they buy.

Again, the best way to use this book is to execute each stage in the sales and marketing process with one (or more) of your own stories. So before you begin this section, pick at least one story you think is ready to send out.

Ready? Let's get started.

CHAPTER 4.
HOW DO I KNOW IT'S READY?:
Submission Fear & Arrogance

BEFORE YOU TRY to "sell" a story, you first need to know if it is in saleable form. So how can you assess whether your story is ready to be submitted to a short fiction market?

Heinlein's Five Rules of Writing

I'd be remiss in writing this book if I didn't mention Robert A. Heinlein's famous (and in one respect, infamous) "Five Rules of Writing":

1. You must write.
2. You must finish what you write.
3. You must refrain from rewriting, except to editorial order.
4. You must put the work on the market.
5. You must keep the work on the market until sold.

These first appeared in Heinlein's 1947 essay "On the Writing of Speculative Fiction," over six decades ago. But they are still quoted today because they remain as true now as when Heinlein coined them in the golden age of the science fiction pulp magazines.

And they remain true for *all* writers, whatever their genre and whether they are wannabes, beginners, or established pros.

To explain these rules, I'll point you to an excellent discussion by multi-award winning SF author, Robert J. Sawyer on his site at http://www.sfwriter.com/ow05.htm. You can find explanations of Heinlein's Rules in ever so many sites on the web, but Rob's is one of the best. Read it, and then come back here.

Ready? Okay. The first two of Heinlein's Rules relate to the creative side of writing—the side that produces your stories. The last three address the business side of being a writer. Those three focus on marketing your fiction with a goal of selling it—or in other words, the scope of this book. So we'll be concentrating on Rules #3-5 in the balance of Section Two.

The Infamous Rule #3

I mentioned that Heinlein's Rules are also infamous in one respect. As Rob Sawyer pointed out in his discussion, the controversy surrounds Rule #3.

> 3. You must refrain from rewriting, except to editorial order.

If taken literally, this seems to advise to not spend any time with editing your stories. I agree with Rob's interpretation that Heinlein was aiming Rule #3 at beginning writers who never finish a story because they are always revising and tweaking it with a goal of making it "perfect." In other words, they are behaving like our Fearful Beginner from Chapter One.

News flash for newbies: your story will *never* be perfect. Period. End of discussion. The story you put on paper (okay, on the screen) will never measure up to your vision for that story that sits in your head, all perfect and pristine.

But don't you want your story to be as good as it can be? As close to perfect as possible?

Yes, you do. And therein lies the problem for beginners and the main challenge in being a professional writer—knowing when your story is "good enough"—knowing when it's ready for the market.

Balancing Fear and Arrogance

A work of art, they say, is never finished—but merely abandoned at an interesting point. Professional writers know when they've reached that point. A beginner invariably struggles with when to stop editing. They fall on one side or the other of the sweet spot: not enough revision or too much. In other words, they will be either Arrogant or the Fearful Beginner.

The Arrogant Beginner bangs out a draft and sends it to a market, maybe after (at most) giving it a quick reread and doing a spell check. They are the writers who don't think they need to learn their craft, or to paraphrase Dean Wesley Smith, the writers who believe "their poop don't smell." They will never sell their stories, because their work will never become good enough to sell until they spend time on practising and learning their craft.

The Fearful Beginner, on the other hand, is the writer at whom Heinlein's Rule #3 is aimed. They're the writer who revises and revises and revises, effectively never finishing a story (and so, technically, never even completing Rule #2).

So, as a beginning writer, how can you find the right balance? How do you know when your story is ready to be "abandoned at an interesting point?" How do you know when it's "good enough" to send out into the world in search of a good home?

I wish I had an easy answer. You can look for symptoms in yourself of being either the Arrogant or the Fearful Beginner. Are you editing your story at all? If not, then you're likely our Arrogant Beginner.

Are your edits making your story closer to the vision in your head? Are they making the story stronger? Then make those changes. But if your edits are only making your story *different*, or if you're not sure if a story is stronger after an edit, then you're suffering from fear.

At that point, you're not improving your story. More likely, you're hurting it. As you try to "polish" your tale to perfection, you are stripping any originality of voice from your prose and blunting any edge in your writing.

A Suggested Approach

Still not helping? Okay, try the following approach. I call it "Three Strikes and Out" (as in *out* to market):

- *Strike One:* Write your draft. And write it in whatever way you wish. Some writers swear by banging out that first draft and never doing any editing until it's done. Others write a bit, edit a bit, write the next part, edit that (that's me, by the way). There is no single "right" way to write. Just do the draft the way you like to write, until you have a completed story.

- Set it aside for a week. No exceptions. No cheating. Your brain needs to distance itself from any memory of the story and the prose. Give it this time, so when you return to the story, you can read it objectively and as fresh as a new reader.

- *Strike Two:* Reread your story, but as a *reader* not an editor. That is, read for enjoyment. But as you read, make notes of what jars you or makes you cringe. Highlight points that are unclear or don't feel right. You're looking for whatever doesn't jive with the vision of the story in your head. And, of course, you can note typos, rough spots of prose, etc. as well.

- Make those changes to the manuscript. If it needs a lot of work, you might need to redraft instead of revising — start again with a blank screen, instead of trying to tweak a manuscript that simply isn't working.

- Set the revised manuscript aside for a week again. And again, no cheating.

- *Strike Three:* Reread the story again, but this time as an editor, critically. Make note of any final changes you want to make. Make those changes, along with a spelling and an intelligent grammar check ("intelligent" means *you* decide, not the word processing program, on what grammar changes are needed. I ignore probably 95% of anything the grammar checker flags).

- *And Out:* You're done. Your story is ready to send out. No, really. It's ready.

This approach is aimed at the Fearful Beginner who keeps breaking Heinlein's third rule. But it will also help the Arrogant Beginner who doesn't spend enough time editing their draft.

And in case it's not obvious, during those days where you're setting this story aside, you should be writing or editing other stories. As you'll learn, writing is a numbers game, a game won by the writer with the most stories written and circulating at the correct markets.

So we've now reached a point where you have a story ready to be submitted to a real market! Congratulations! Next, we'll discuss how to send your story out into the world (and how not to).

CHAPTER 5.

WHERE TO FIRST?:

A Strategy for Choosing Short Fiction Markets

In Chapter Four, you learned Robert A. Heinlein's famous "Five Rules of Writing":

1. You must write.
2. You must finish what you write.
3. You must refrain from rewriting, except to editorial order.
4. You must put the work on the market.
5. You must keep the work on the market until sold.

This book focuses on Rules #3-5. In the last chapter, we discussed the controversial Rule #3 along with tips on how to follow that rule. The balance of Section Two will focus on Rules #4-5.

Where to Submit First?

So we've reached a point where you've finished a story to your satisfaction and are ready to submit it to a market. You're now facing your first and perhaps most critical marketing decision. Where should you send your story *first*?

The emphasis on "first" should be obvious, assuming you've read Chapter Three on understanding rights and licensing for short fiction. You can only sell "first rights" to a story once, so you want to sell those valuable first rights to the very best market possible. This leads me to what is probably the most important piece of advice I can give on selling short fiction:

Start at the top.

What does that mean? Simple: *find the very best market you can and send your story there first.* Period. End of lecture.

Okay, not the end. Not the end because, although it's simple and obvious advice, new writers often balk at following it, especially the Fearful Beginners.

Self-Rejecting Writers

Why do they balk? Simple. They lack belief in themselves and in their work. They'll say "I'm just a beginner" or "I'm not very good" or "It's my first story." Or they'll give another self-diminishing reason, followed by their conclusion that no top market would possibly ever buy their work.

This is self-rejection and is based on a flawed premise. To quote multi-genre, multi-award winning writer, Kristine Kathryn Rusch, "you are the worst judge of your own work." Kris and Dean Wesley Smith drive this point home in their short fiction workshops where you submit three stories that include, in *your* opinion, your best and your worst. An exercise follows where workshop participants create an anthology built from those submitted stories. Guess what? Your "worst" story is generally picked by your fellow workshop members for their anthologies as frequently as your presumed "best" story.

Editorial Need

The other argument against self-rejection is editorial need. You have no idea what the editor of that top market you're avoiding needs for their anthology or for the next issue of their magazine.

A beginning writer once told the famous science fiction writer and editor, John W. Campbell, he had never submitted a story to Campbell's *Astounding Science Fiction* (later *Analog*) because he didn't think his writing was good enough. Campbell responded with an indignant, "How dare you do my job for me!"

Exactly. Your opinion means nothing. Only the editor's opinion counts. So send them your stories and send only to the best markets!

What If You Don't Start at the Top?

If you're still not convinced, then play this scenario through in your head. Imagine you've written your first story, have made it as good as you possibly can, and are now ready to try to sell it.

Let's say you *don't* follow my advice. Pretend you send your story to a semi-pro market or worse still, a market that pays in "exposure" (Another term I hate. The only exposure you'll get from submitting to one of those markets is exposing yourself as a naive beginner. You want exposure? Then sell to a top market.).

Now pretend you *do* sell it to that lower market. Imagine yourself opening that acceptance letter / email. Imagine your reaction. Excited? Happy? Sure...

At first.

But I guarantee your next feeling is going to be *doubt*. A little nagging thought will appear in the back of your mind: "Gee, if *they* bought it, I wonder if I could have sold it to a *better* market?" As you think about that, your initial thrill will slip away, soon to be replaced by a sick ache in your gut.

And guess what? You'll *never* know. You'll never find out if this story could have launched your career by appearing in *Asimov's* or *Analog* or *The Magazine of Fantasy & Science Fiction* or any other top market. You'll never find out because you've thrown away your *only* chance to sell first rights to that story. Top markets don't buy second rights.

What Do You Have to Lose?

If you submit to a top market and *don't* sell it, what have you lost? Nothing, aside from time (we'll talk more about submission time in an upcoming chapter).

And no, if the editor at that top market rejects your story, they will not record a "black mark" against you (another oft-mentioned and equally silly fear of beginners). They won't even remember you, unless your story came close, which is a good thing. These markets get hundreds and hundreds of submissions each month, most of which are read by slush readers, not the editor. I guarantee they forget a rejected story immediately.

One last argument for "start at the top"—if you do sell to a lower level, non-pro market, nobody will care. *Nobody.* Sales to those markets won't impress established pros. They won't impress editors at the big markets either. We'll learn in Chapter Eight that you should never include sales to non-pro markets in your cover letters. You'll just underscore that you're a beginner.

So what have you gained by selling to a lower, non-pro market? Absolutely nothing.

So don't do it.

Defining a Top Market

Assuming I've convinced you to start at the top, how do we define *top*? Ultimately, that definition depends on *your* goals as a writer (see Chapter One). But for me, a top market means the following:

- They pay "professional" rates: For speculative fiction markets, the Science Fiction & Fantasy Writers of America (SFWA) set criteria for professional payment. As of July 2014, this is a minimum of six cents USD per word. Yeah, that sucks. You will not be quitting your day job even when you start selling short stories.

- They have a good reputation: A sale to this market will look good on your resume and will impress pros and editors.

- They publish stories that consistently show up on the major award lists: Check out past winners of the Hugo, Nebula and other awards. You can find a list of major and minor SF&F awards on my website at smithwriter.com/more_links_for_ writers under "Awards."

- They offer other benefits important to you personally: For example, I love the semi-pro Canadian magazine, *On Spec*. I like their taste in fiction and how they treat their writers. Plus, hey, I'm a Canadian. So *On Spec* is on my submission list, whereas it might not be on yours. They're not at the top, but they're on my personal list.

Your Best to the Best

Yes, I've spent an entire chapter trying to convince you to send your short fiction to the very best market you can find first. That alone should tell you how important that advice is to any writer planning to use their short fiction to help build a writing career. You've worked hard to make your story the best you can, right? So why would you offer your best to anyone less than the best?

CHAPTER 6.
WHERE TO LOOK:
Finding Short Fiction Markets

You NOW KNOW to "start at top" when deciding where to first send a story. That means starting with the very best markets and working down your list until you get a sale. A top market is defined as one that pays professional rates, publishes stories that regularly appear on award ballots, and has a good cachet in the business.

In this chapter, we look at online resources for identifying available short fiction markets, and how to use them to select your list of top markets.

Magazines versus Anthologies

As mentioned in Chapter Three, two types of markets exist that buy first rights for short fiction:

- Magazines (either print and/or electronic, where electronic could be a web-based magazine or one provided in ebook or PDF format); and,

- Anthologies (again, either print and/or electronic).

It bears repeating since so many beginners confuse the terms. An *anthology* is a book-length work that contains stories from *different* authors. A *collection* is a book-length work that contains stories from a *single* author. The terms are *not* interchangeable. We discuss publishing a collection of your short fiction later in Section Four. Before you can publish a collection, you need to have both sold many short stories and built a name for yourself. So let's start you on that road.

Between magazines and anthologies, my personal choice is to first focus on the big professional magazine markets, including *Asimov's*, *Analog*, *Magazine of Fantasy & SF*, *Ellery Queen*, and *Alfred Hitchcock*. I'll send to other non-genre top markets before these, but you should understand they are a harder sell, in general and for genre in particular. These include *The New Yorker*, *Playboy*, *Glimmer Train*, and the Carus Publishing age-bracketed magazines such as *Cricket* and *Cicada*. All of these magazines meet the criteria for a top market.

I send to the top magazines before anthologies because of the visibility a sale to those magazines brings, in terms of award potential and looking good on your resume. I'll consider anthologies after I run out of the top magazines. The exceptions are anthologies with a high profile editor or in a well-regarded series (the cachet factor on your writing resume). I'll also consider starting with an anthology if the anthology's theme is a very good fit for my story and my story is a little off-beat, meaning it might have a hard time finding a home in a magazine.

Finding the Markets: Ralan.com

The good news for short fiction writers is that several excellent and free market resources exist on the web. In my opinion, the best market list for speculative fiction markets is www.ralan.com, a site maintained by writer Ralan Conley. Since 1994 it has consistently been the go-to, one-stop-shopping place to find current short fiction genre markets: science fiction, fantasy, horror, mystery, slipstream, etc. (but not so much romance). And it's free.

Yes, other market lists exist, but I've relied on Ralan's list since I started writing. A market may from time to time appear first in another market list, but Ralan will add it very quickly. Save yourself time and effort—get to know Ralan's list and visit it regularly.

Ralan's site is organized into separate pages based on pay rate (pro, semi-pro, etc.) and market format (magazines, anthologies, audio etc.). Ignore the audio markets for now. We'll discuss selling audio and other rights to your stories in Section Four. For now, we are focusing on selling *first print rights* (either physical print or electronic print), so you should focus on magazines and anthologies.

Ralan separates magazines into professional (paying at least SFWA rates), semi-professional (at least 3 cents per word but less than SFWA rates), pay (1-2 cents per word), token (less than 1 cent per word), and exposure (no pay—and no exposure either, because no one reads these publications).

So how should you use Ralan's site? For a first rights sale, you're only interested in the top markets, remember? That means you want markets that pay at least the pro rate, which means you need to look at just two of Ralan's pages:

- Professional magazines (www.ralan.com/m.pro.htm); and,

- Anthologies (www.ralan.com/m.antho.htm). For this page, ignore the anthologies that pay below professional rates. We'll come back to lower paying anthologies in Section Four, when we discuss reprint markets.

Other Genre Lists

I'll mention a couple of other genre market lists. One is Duotrope (duotrope.com), which originally was a free and popular service. You now need a paid subscription to access their list of markets. Duotrope also offers the ability to search markets based on different factors, such as pay rate, genre, word length, and whether they take reprints.

Another market list is The Grinder (http://thegrinder.diabolicalplots. com), with a search feature similar to Duotrope. But unlike Duotrope, The Grinder is (at time of writing) a free service.

Personally, I've never found a search feature to be that useful. Professional markets aren't that numerous, so becoming familiar with them is not a huge challenge. If you plan to be a professional writer, then you need to spend the time and effort to learn your markets. Review Ralan's list and then check out the online magazines or purchase sample copies for the print magazines (many of which now offer ebook editions).

Ralan also posts new markets and updates at the top of each category page, so once you've learned a market list, it's easy to keep up with changes by simply checking his site once a month.

Literary (Non-Genre) Markets

If you write mainstream short fiction and are interested in literary (non-genre) markets, then you should check out www.pw.org/literary_magazines. This list provides a search feature with a filter to select markets based on their format (print, web, etc.), genre (in this case, fiction vs. poetry), and most importantly, paying vs. non-paying (the payment feature is under "more filter options").

Submission Tracking

A popular feature that both Duotrope and The Grinder offer is a submission tracker. We'll cover submission tracking in detail in Chapter Ten, including free software options in addition to those two sites. Right now, focus on getting your first story out to the right market. But understand that once you have multiple stories circulating, you *will* need a process or tool to track your submissions and their status, or you'll get into *big* trouble.

Picking the Right Market

So now you have resources to identify the professional markets out there along with rules to develop your own list of top markets. Next, we'll discuss how to choose which of the top markets on your personal list is the *best* fit for your story.

CHAPTER 7.
MARKETS, MARKETS EVERYWHERE:
Selecting the *Right* Market

IN CHAPTER FIVE, we learned why you must "start at the top" when deciding where to first send a story, meaning starting with the very best markets available. In Chapter Six, we reviewed market list sources available on the web and how to use them to develop your own personalized list of top markets.

In this chapter, you'll learn how to select which top markets on your personal list are the *best* fit for the particular story you're planning to submit.

How to Pick the Right Market

Use your chosen market list (Ralan, Duotrope, etc.) to access the market's website and find their *submission guidelines* page. Submission guidelines (or GLs for short), if they're well written, provide five important types of information about a market:

1. A summary of the rights they will want to license from you;
2. The payment they offer for those rights;
3. The types of stories they publish, including genres and sub-genres;
4. The maximum word length they will consider for a story (and sometimes, minimum and preferred lengths); and,
5. How to submit a story for their consideration.

Rights

First, make sure you understand exactly what rights you will be giving up (and for how long) if you sell to this market. We dealt with understanding rights in Chapter Three, so I'm not going to repeat any of that here. Read that chapter if you haven't yet—as I said, it contains the most important information in this book for a writer.

Remember your top markets will be those that acquire *first* rights. Be aware some markets take only reprints (second rights). We'll deal with reprint markets in detail in Section Four. For now, just make sure you never submit a never-sold story to a reprint-only market, or a previously sold story to a first rights only market.

Payment

Since it's on your "top markets" list, the market you've selected will be paying professional rates, right? Right?

If the market is asking for more than minimum rights, you need to decide if the payment or cachet for selling to this market is worth giving up the additional rights. Your story, your career, your decision.

Another consideration is the timing of payment. Most markets pay "on publication"—after your story is physically published in the magazine or anthology. Less commonly, a few pay "on acceptance"— when they accept your story for publication, a bonus for the writer.

Finally, for first rights sales, stay away from markets offering only royalty payments based on the number of copies sold. These tend to be anthologies, and trust me, they will never pay a professional rate in the end, and may not ever pay you anything.

Types of Stories Published: Genre

Before submitting to your selected target market, you *must* ensure your story is a good fit in genre, style, and tone to the type of stories that market publishes. Let's cover genre first.

The most common genres in the speculative short fiction markets are science fiction, fantasy, and horror. Many markets publish all three. Some focus only on one. Some narrow their genre focus even further (hard SF, space exploration SF, alternate history, dark fantasy, urban fantasy, supernatural horror, etc.). Mystery and crime are other common and healthy short fiction genres.

Never submit a story outside the genre your target market publishes. That market has a specific audience as subscribers, and if that audience wants high fantasy, that editor will not buy your urban fantasy.

I'm frequently surprised by how many new writers do not understand genre, or even worse, cannot correctly identify the genre of a story they've written. The only way to understand genre differences is to read widely across the spectrum of speculative fiction. If you want a starting point for understanding the various genres, subgenres, and their characteristics, check out this site: www.cuebon.com/ewriters/definitions.html.

Even if your story matches the market's preferred genre, you still need to be sure it's a fit for style and tone. The guidelines may help, but you'll generally need to get a sample copy or two and read the kinds of stories they publish. Do they seem to prefer character or plot-driven stories? Optimistic or pessimistic? Dark? Humorous? Literary prose styles? In short, does this market *feel* like a good fit for the story you've written?

Yes, this requires more work. But if these are the markets where you will target your stories, then isn't it worth the effort to understand the type of fiction they publish?

Types of Stories Published: Theme

You'll usually find it easier to decide if a story is a fit to an anthology than to a magazine, since most anthologies are *themed*, meaning they are looking only for stories around a particular topic. Some magazines occasionally publish themed issues as well.

Themed markets can be cross-genre or genre-specific. Some anthologies to which I've sold had such themes as apocalypses (cross-genre), Japan (fantasies only), circuses (fantasies), werewolves (fantasies, in case you hadn't figured that out), and resource wars (cross-genre).

Themed markets are generally feast or famine for a writer. If your story fits, you'll have a better chance of selling than with a generic market, because a theme narrows the competition. The narrower the theme, the better chance of a sale if you fit the theme, assuming your story is written at a professional level.

Just be wary of very narrowly themed anthologies. Such projects also present the highest probability of delays before publication or of never getting published, since they face the greatest difficulties finding enough quality stories to fill a book.

Another warning about anthologies: make sure a publisher has committed to putting out the book. Sometimes a wannabe editor starts collecting stories before they've sold the anthology to a publisher. Remember it's the publisher that pays contributing writers, not the editor.

Types of Stories Published: Length

Most markets specify a maximum length in words for stories they will consider. Do *not* exceed that maximum. You'll only irritate the editor and win a quick trip to the rejection pile. Once you've sold a few or get to know a particular editor, you can sometimes ask them if they'd consider a longer work. But don't try that as a beginner.

While we're talking about story length, here's a critical piece of advice for selling short fiction:

Shorter is better.

Let's say you have a 6,000-word story, and you know a pro market that specifies a maximum word count of 6,000. Yes, you can send your story there, but you'll have a harder time selling that story than if you sent a 3,000-word story to the same market.

Why? Think about it. Editors have a maximum number of total words of fiction they can afford to publish in any magazine issue or anthology. Yes, there's some flexibility, but not a lot. If an editor has a choice of publishing two good 3,000-word stories or one good 6,000-word story (yours), they're going to go with the two shorter stories.

Why? Because that decision gives their readers more stories, plus if a reader doesn't enjoy the first story, they might like the second. Picking a single, longer story is a higher risk choice for an editor. For you as a writer, this means the *longer* your story is, the *better* it has to be.

A Word on Contests

I discourage new writers from submitting to any market that requires the writer to pay to submit, and that includes most contests. In general, folks, remember this rule:

Money flows to the writer.

If you need to pay money to submit your story, either to enter a contest or for a "reading fee," don't submit to that market. Most contests are just money-making exercises for the market, and reading fees a way to keep the slush pile smaller (more on the slush pile in Chapter Eleven).

No, not all contests are simply money grabs, but as a beginning writer you are far better targeting the top markets. Trust me, a sale to a professional market or anthology will look much better in your cover letter than a win in some contest.

Homework

If you're applying the guidance from this book as you go, then by now you should have used the resources provided in Chapter Six to compile your list of top markets that fit your kind of writing and your goals as a writer. Now I want you to use the information in

51

this chapter to filter through that list and pick the single best market to *first* submit your story.

Why? Because in the next chapter, you'll learn how to submit your story to your selected market, including what to put in a cover letter and how to format a manuscript.

CHAPTER 8.
DEAR EDITOR:
How to Submit Short Fiction

In Chapters Five and Six, we reviewed market lists and an approach to develop your own list of top markets to target for your stories. In Chapter Seven, we looked at how to select which of the top markets on your personal list is the *best* fit for the story you plan to submit. Now, let's discuss the mechanics of submitting your story to the target market you've now selected.

The Common Ways of Submitting

The submission guidelines page of your target market's website will explain the specific process to follow when sending a story to that market. For the vast majority of markets, this process will be one of the following:

- By email, with a cover letter in the body of the email and the story attached as a specified type of file;

- By email, with both the cover letter *and* the story in the body of the email;

- An online form, where you cut and paste your cover letter and story into the form;

- An online submission system, such as Submittable, where you type your cover letter into a form, and then upload your story as a specified type of file; or,

- By snail mail; that is, physically mailing a printed copy of the story and cover letter (yes, dinosaurs still roam the Earth).

The most common current method is by email with an attachment, but online submission systems are becoming more prevalent. These systems often send you a confirmation of receipt and allow you to track the progress of your submission online.

The market's guidelines will give specific instructions on how to submit. I shouldn't need to say this, but given the number of editors who complain about this, I will:

Follow a market's instructions for submitting exactly.

If they ask for the story pasted into the body of the email, and you send it as an attachment, you'll win a quick trip to the delete folder for your story.

And if they take attachments, send only the type of attachments they specify. Many will *not* accept .docx files out of MS-Word, but will accept .doc files. RTF (rich text format) files are accepted by most markets that take attachments, but *always read the guidelines*.

The Dreaded Snail Mail Market

If a market only takes postal submissions, their submission guidelines will include something along the lines of "Please include a SASE with your submission if you wish a reply."

SASE (pronounced "sassy") means Self-Addressed Stamped Envelope—an unsealed, letter-size (a #9 or #10 works) envelope with *your* address typed neatly on the front *and* with the correct postage affixed to it. "Correct" postage means both the amount and the country. I'm in Canada, so when I submit to a snail mail market in the US, I need to attach sufficient *US stamps* (not Canadian) to my SASE for international mail from the US to Canada. You can check current postal rates online for the following English-speaking countries:

- Canada: www.canadapost.ca
- USA: www.usps.com
- Australia: auspost.com.au
- United Kingdom: www.royalmail.com

So how do you get stamps from another country? One way is to have a friend living in that country buy them and mail them to you. You can also order them via most of the above websites. If you live in a large city, you may be able to find a stamp and coin store that sells foreign stamps, although you'll pay more since they need to make a profit.

Another option, especially for overseas markets, is to include an SAE (Self-Addressed Envelope, with no postage attached) along with an IRC (International Reply Coupon). You can buy IRCs in most post offices. They act like a voucher that can be exchanged for postage in the market's country. It may sound easier, but be warned—they are expensive.

You can sometimes avoid the need for a SASE if the guidelines state they will respond to your submission by email. Just be sure to include your email on your cover letter and manuscript cover page.

If you want the market to also return your manuscript, then your SASE needs to be large enough to hold your manuscript (and with much more postage). My strong advice is *not* to ask for the return of your manuscript. Aside from the postage cost, after a few rejections, your much-traveled manuscript will look much rejected—not the first impression you want to make on the next editor.

All this adds up to snail mail markets being a pain for submissions, which is why I'm glad the number of these markets has dwindled.

Cover Letters

No matter what method a market uses for submissions, you need to include a cover letter, which provides your next opportunity for making a bad impression.

Here is a sample cover letter based on one of my recent submissions:

> Dear <editor's name>:
>
> Please find <attached / enclosed / below> my 5,100-word story "Gypsy Biker" for consideration for <market name>. This story has not been previously published.

My stories have appeared in thirty countries and twenty-five languages, including *InterZone*, *Weird Tales*, *Amazing Stories*, *The Mammoth Book of Best New Horror*, and *Cicada*, as well as numerous professional anthologies. My book-length works include a novel, *The Wolf at the End of the World*, and three collections, *Chimerascope* (ChiZine Publications), *Impossibilia* (PS Publishing), and *La Danse des Esprits* (Dreampress, France). I have won the Aurora Award three times and have been a finalist for the John W. Campbell Award, the juried Sunburst Award, the CBC Bookies Award, and France's juried Prix Masterton and Prix Bob Morane.

Thank you for your consideration. I look forward to your response.

Sincerely,

Douglas Smith

www.smithwriter.com

Now, let's go over the above sample, noting the important points:

- For <editor name>, put their actual surname with the appropriate title: "Ms. Jones" or "Mr. Brown." You'll find their name on the website and usually on the guidelines page.

- Another view on <editor name>. Many editors these days are recommending simply using the editor's first and last names ("Mary Jones") without any honorific (Mr., Ms.), to avoid a possibly inappropriate (to the editor) gender or marital implication. Using an editor's first and last names maintains the required level of formality and is still well-received.

- More on <editor name>. If—*and only if*—you know the editor personally (from a convention, from a prior acceptance, from regular correspondence), you can use their first name: "Dear Ellen" or "Dear David". Use your common sense—don't be familiar if you haven't earned it.

- And still more on <editor name>. If you can't find the editor's name, avoid at all costs simply saying "Dear editor" or "Dear sir or madam." Many editors will interpret this (and rightly so) as a sign that you are not reading their magazine and were unwilling to do your market research. Not the first impression you wish to make on an editor. That will earn you a quick trip to the rejection pile, or at best, to the bottom of the slush pile.

- Since we're dealing with selling first rights at this point, the declaration the story has not been previously published is redundant, but it doesn't hurt. I'll be dealing with cover letters for reprints later.

- If *this* editor has bought a story from you before, mention that in your first paragraph in a personalized way: "I was thrilled to see my story "Gerbils from Space" in the Winter 2014 issue of *Awesome Stories*. Thanks again for buying it." If you've sold to this *market* (but not this editor), then just say something like: "I am a previous contributor to *Awesome Stories* (Winter 2014 issue)."

- If you *have* publication credits, only include professional and highly regarded markets. No matter how proud you are of your sale to some semi-pro or non-paying market (and you shouldn't be submitting to those to start with—read Chapter Five again), including such "credits" will hurt your credibility, not help it. Please trust me on this.

- If you have a *lot* of professional publication credits, select only a few of your best. I obviously didn't list all of my credits in the above sample. Some editors suggest a maximum of five or six.

- If you've won or been short-listed (on the final voting ballot) for any major or regional awards, include that as well.

- If you don't yet have any professional publications credits or awards, *just drop the second paragraph.* Don't worry—editors are buying your story, not your resume.

- If you have any special credentials *relevant to the story*, then you can include them. An example might be that you're an emergency room doctor, and your story is a medical thriller.

What *Not* to Include in a Cover Letter

What shouldn't you include in a cover letter? The simple answer is anything beyond what I show in the above example. But since editors still cite common mistakes in cover letters, I'll list the more brain-dead examples:

- Do not try to describe or summarize your story. Sorry, but your story must do that for itself, just as it will for a reader if this editor publishes it.

- Don't bother trying to identify the genre or sub-genre of your story in your cover letter. You're probably wrong, the editor doesn't care, and if you've done a good job in selecting the market based on what they publish, then it doesn't matter. And if you haven't, it's too late.

- Do *not* include your membership in any professional writers association (e.g., "SFWA member"). No one cares, especially an editor. More importantly, for some editors, this is a strong negative and a sign of an *un*professional writer. Professionals don't need to list the associations they belong to.

- Unless you have a personal relationship with this editor, do *not* talk about your personal life. If the editor doesn't know you personally, they don't care. No, really—they don't care. Especially, don't talk about your cats.

- The flip side is true as well. If you *do* know the editor personally, you should include something to reflect that relationship. Just don't go overboard. Editors are busy people (but human, too).

- Do not tell the editor how this story idea came to you or why you wrote it ("This story was inspired by the tragic death of my possum, Clyde..."). Again, no one cares. Except maybe Clyde (and he's dead).

- Do not tell the editor how you wrote this story or the pain involved in its birth. More not caring involved.

- Most particularly, do not explain how your <spouse / mother / BFF / kids / cat / possum> love this story. Awesome amounts of not caring for this one.

- Worth repeating: No cats. Or possums.

Basically, your cover letter is as follows:

"Here's my story. It's this long. Here are my credits. Thanks for listening."

That's it. That's *all* you need. If you add more, you're probably making a mistake.

Manuscript Formatting for Short Fiction

Much has been written on how to properly format a short story manuscript. I won't add to the surfeit here. Instead, I'll point you to two of the better sites:

Proper Manuscript Format, from SF author, William Shunn: www. shunn.net/format/story.html

Manuscript Formatting Checklist, from award-winning SF author, Robert J. Sawyer: www.sfwriter.com/mschklst.htm

Shunn's site provides a sample of a formatted manuscript, which he uses to explain the various rules along with the reasons for those rules. Rob Sawyer's site is a good summary as well, plus Rob includes instructions on setting the recommended formatting in Word.

Both are excellent sites, but I'll suggest a few modifications of my own to their recommendations:

On Shunn's list:

- As mentioned under cover letters, do *not* include your membership in any professional writers association (e.g., "SFWA member") on the first page of your manuscript.

- Use *exactly* one inch margins, not "at least".

- Always, always, always include a clear indicator to mark the end of your story, either "##" (the accepted standard) or "The End"

On Rob's list:

- "Disposable manuscript" is not required for snail mail submissions anymore (and obviously not for email subs). If you don't include a large envelope for the return of the manuscript, "disposable" is assumed.

- Using "—30—" at the end is more common for journalists, not short fiction writers. Use "##" instead.

On both lists:

- Use *italics*, not <u>underlining</u>, to indicate text you want in *italics*. The use of underlining for italics is no longer the accepted practice for the vast majority of markets. In fact, many markets now explicitly request in their guidelines that you do *not* do this, especially markets that accept electronic submissions. Changing underlining to italics is extra work for an editor if you've already submitted an electronic file. So: show *italicized text* in *italics*.

A final note on manuscript formatting—always check the market's submission guidelines and follow those guidelines *exactly* when you submit, even if they contradict anything I've written here. The editor is always right.

Internal Dialog

One topic not mentioned on the above sites is how to format *internal* dialog—the thoughts a character is having. My preference is to use italics. For example:

"John!" came a greeting from behind him.

He turned to see Sally Turner striding towards him. *Oh, crap, he thought. Just what I need right now.*

The italics in the above indicate a dialog the character is having with himself. Note that this internal dialog is in *present* tense even though the scene is written in past tense.

I could rewrite the above passage without internal dialog but still imparting the same information:

"John!" came a greeting from behind him.

He turned to see Sally Turner striding towards him. He swore to himself. Sally was the last person he needed to meet today.

I've replaced the internal dialog here with a description of the character's thoughts, not the thoughts themselves, so the italics are not needed. Note that the revised sentences are written in past tense, just like the rest of the scene.

Paranormal Dialog

If you write fantasy or science fiction, it's possible you will have situations involving telepathy, which is just another form of dialog. The easiest way is to use italics again, making it clear these thoughts are a conversation between characters and not internal thoughts by one character:

"John!" came a greeting from behind them.

He and Renita turned to see Sally Turner striding towards them.

Oh, crap, he swore. *She's the last thing we need right now.*

Let me handle her, Renita replied.

You can also use special formatting, like enclosing telepathy in diamond brackets (<Oh, crap!>), but remember this has to be translated into a magazine or book. If you can make italics work, it's the easiest for a reader to interpret.

Formatting Plain Text

Typically, the only formatting you need in a short story is italics. However, some markets use online form submission systems, which often only allow plain text. That is, they don't allow any special formatting such as underlining, italics, or bolding.

So how do you indicate text that should be italicized in the final publication?

In a plain text version of a manuscript, underlining is shown by preceding and following the text to be italicized by an underscore character. So to underline (italicize) the word "wolf," you type it as _wolf_. Bolding (not typically done in fiction) is done by using an asterisk around the text to be bolded, such as *wolf*.

Word Count: A Brief History Lesson

For many years, the accepted way of calculating the number of words in your manuscript was as follows:

- Format your manuscript as described earlier in this chapter: double-spaced, 1" margins, non-proportional font at 12 point / 10 pitch. This formatting should produce twenty-five lines per printed page.

- Assume an average of ten words per line, giving a standard of two hundred and fifty words per full manuscript page.

- (a) Count the number of *full* pages (pages with 25 lines). This is usually the total pages minus two, since the cover page (always) and final page (usually) have less than twenty-five lines; (b) multiply the number of full pages by twenty-five; (c) add the number of lines on the first and last pages; (d) multiply that number (the total number of lines in the story) by 10 (the standard assumed average number of words per line).

Example: for a properly formatted 23-page story, with eleven lines on the first page and three on the final page (not counting "The End"), the word count would be: $(((23-2) \times 25) + 11 + 3)) * 10 = 5,390$, which you would then round up to 5,400 words. Always round your word counts to the nearest 100 words.

Um, okay, you say. But why not just use the word count your word processing package gives you?

Well, first, editors developed the above method before word processing packages existed to have a quick and consistent way to estimate word count. Second, for print magazines, the important aspect about the length of a story isn't its *word* length, but rather its *physical* length—how much column space this story will take up in the actual magazine. And for that, line count is more accurate than word count. Consider the following exchange:

"You okay?"

"No."

Only three words, yet they still require two lines. A print magazine editor needs to know how much space the stories in an issue will take up, to know how much space is left over for advertising, illustrations, editorials, and reviews. So those three words above would be counted as twenty (two lines x ten words).

Word Count: The Modern (and Accepted) Method

History aside, most markets today expect you to use the word count from your word processor, since few writers now use anything else. The advent of online magazines, where physical layout is less an issue, has also driven this in part.

Easier for you, right? Sure, but not as profitable. The word processor count will almost always be lower than the count from the traditional method (see my example above where the editor counted three words as twenty). Since you're paid on a *per word rate*, you'll receive less using the word processor count—another reason most markets now accept a computer word count.

But regardless, you no longer have a choice. So for word count, use the number that your word processing software provides.

If you're one of the remaining dinosaurs who still uses a typewriter, you can use the old method, but the market will eventually have to put your story into an electronic form, and then they'll just pay you based on the electronic word count anyway.

Homework

You are now ready to apply what you've learned in this chapter. Before we proceed any further, I want you to take one of your stories that is ready for market and to prepare your submission package: a cover letter and a properly formatted manuscript.

But don't send it out yet. Before we leave this topic of submitting stories, we need to cover two common submission mistakes beginners make that can get you into a lot of trouble.

CHAPTER 9.
THE NO-NOS:
What *Not* to Do When Submitting Fiction

IN THE LAST chapter, we discussed how to submit your story to a market, including different submission methods, cover letters, manuscript formatting, formatting different types of dialog, and an explanation of the two methods of calculating word count.

In this chapter, we finish the topic on how to submit short fiction by discussing two commonly confused and unwise practices: multiple submissions and simultaneous submissions.

Multiple Submissions: Not a Good Idea

A *multiple submission* means submitting *more than one story* to the *same market* at the *same time*. Don't confuse this with the horrible and evil *simultaneous submission*, which we cover later in this chapter.

Even if a market accepts multiple submissions (that is, you can send that market two or more stories at a time), my very strong advice is not to do so, especially for magazines. It is very unlikely a magazine would buy more than one story at once from you, especially if you're a beginner with no name value.

Why? Most magazines don't build up an inventory of stories—they buy for the next issue and no further. Yes, some magazines do buy for future issues, but you need to deal with the *majority* of cases. If you send four stories to a market, and they buy one and reject three, you've lost your chance to sell them those three rejected stories for a future issue.

Anthologies are a different case. Most anthologies are one-time only with a specific theme and a submission deadline. Therefore, if an anthology allows multiple submissions, there's no downside in sending more than one story, assuming all the stories you send fit their theme and guidelines. But be reasonable—no more than three at once, and a maximum of two is better.

However, for *recurring* anthologies, I'd again recommend against multiple submissions. The editor will buy at most one story from you for this volume of the anthology. Your other stories will be rejected, losing you the chance to submit them to the next volume in the series.

Simultaneous Submissions: The Ultimate No-No

A simultaneous submission means sending the same story to more than one market at the same time.

Here's a simple rule, folks. Learn this and never ever break it:

> *DO NOT* EVER *SUBMIT THE SAME STORY TO MORE THAN ONE MARKET AT ONCE.*

Yes, that was all in caps.

Yes, I'm yelling at you.

Beginning writers obsess about making some career-ending mistake when submitting their fiction. They stress over cover letters and fonts and word counts and formats and a thousand little things they fear will place them on an imagined "black list" they believe all editors keep, written presumably in the blood of new writers foolish enough to make any of these errors.

Trust me, you can stop worrying. None of those things matter (well, not much), and none will get you on an editor's black list (yes, they do have lists, but most are not written in blood).

Simultaneous submissions (sim subs, for short), however, will get you on their black list big time. Why? Well, if you sim sub, you introduce the possibility more than one market will want to buy that story.

Great! you say.

Um, no. You now have a problem. A very big problem. You now must tell one of those editors your story is no longer available to them (not first rights, anyway).

That editor now must find another quality story to fill their issue or anthology. But they might not *have* another quality story that fits with their anthology's theme or with the other stories in that issue. They liked your story, maybe even *loved* your story.

Now they can't publish it. They have a problem—and one *you* caused them. Trust me, they are not happy—and especially with you.

And if they edit a print magazine, even if they can find another good story, it's unlikely the story will be the same length, which means they must completely redo the physical layout of the issue. Are they even angrier with you? Oh, yeah.

It gets worse. Editors often don't tell authors they're accepting a story until they're close to their publishing deadline, which means they might not have any time to react at all when you pull your story. You are now a few rungs below pond scum in their eyes.

And, yes—you are now on their list, the bad one. You've moved from being on their this-is-a-writer-to-watch good list to their this-is-a-writer-to-avoid black list.

So repeat after me:

NO SIM SUBS. EVER.

But, But, But...

But wait, you say, some markets state in their guidelines they accept simultaneous submissions. So obviously, it's all right to sim sub to them, right?

Maybe.

Why maybe? Think about it. You can only sim sub to multiple markets if *all* those markets accept sim subs.

Let's say you submit your story to two markets, one that takes sim subs and one that doesn't. You still face the same problem described above. If both those editors want to buy your story, you need to tell one of them they can't. In this scenario, you can tell the editor who accepts sim subs that, unfortunately, you've already sold your story to another market.

No big, right? They said they took sim subs, so they must be used to this. Sure, except...

Except you don't control *when* you hear from these editors about your acceptance. If the market that *doesn't* take sim subs contacts you first, with either an acceptance or rejection, then you're okay.

But what if the sim sub market contacts you first, and with an acceptance? You must now contact the non-sim sub editor to tell them you need to withdraw your story. Even if you don't tell them why, they'll know you sim subbed to them. And yes, you're on their bad list now.

What if you just didn't inform the non-sim sub editor your story sold? Just hope they'll reject you so they'll never know you sim subbed? If you do, you'll make things worse if they want to buy your story, since they'll have less time to react to the trouble you've just caused them.

Even if you sim sub solely to markets that take sim subs, it's not going to help you. No top professional market (the ones you're targeting, right?) takes simultaneous submissions. So why bother?

So we're back to my original advice:

NO SIM SUBS. EVER.

CHAPTER 10.

THE NUMBERS GAME:

What to Do after You've Submitted a Story

In CHAPTERS EIGHT and Nine, we reviewed the process for submitting your short fiction to one of your targeted markets and reviewed the key mistakes to avoid. I'll assume you've been following this process and have now submitted one of your stories to the top market on your list.

I've Sent My Story—Now What?

First, congratulations. Good for you. You're on your way. So now you can sit back and wait for the editor to reply to your submission, right?

Wrong (c'mon, you knew that was coming). What is *right* is to *write*. Write another story. Send it out to your *next* top market. Then write *another* story and send it out. Rinse and repeat.

The Secret to Success as a Writer

I bet that heading caught your attention. So here's the secret—the secret to success as a writer, whether as a short fiction writer or as a novelist. Ready? Okay, then.

It's a numbers game.

The more fiction you've written *and* you have out in front of editors at professional markets, the better your chances of success.

That should be obvious, but many new writers send out that first story and then sit back and wait for a reply—a reply that will likely be a rejection. Sorry, but the odds are you're not going to sell your first story to the first market to which you send it. We'll cover handling rejections in Chapter Twelve, but for now, just expect to send your story out several times before you sell it.

My average since I began submitting short fiction is about a sale for every seven submissions. I've averaged a much better rate in recent years, because I'm a better writer, because much of what I write now is in response to invitation-only anthologies, and because my numbers now include reprint sales, which are easier to sell.

But when I started, in my first couple of years, I averaged about *fifteen* rejections before getting a first rights sale.

Do the Math

You learned in Chapter Nine to never do simultaneous submissions, so you need to wait to hear back on any submission before you can send that story out again. How long will the wait be? Most professional markets take, on average, *three months* to reply.

So even if you sell that story after only ten submissions, instead of my average of fifteen when I started, you'll still take thirty months, or *two and a half years* to sell that story. If you just sit back and wait on a single submission, *a quarter of a century* will pass before you sell ten stories, still not even enough for a collection. Get the picture?

You need to write a *lot* of stories and send them out as soon as they're ready. You must develop your list of multiple top markets. And you must keep your stories in front of those markets, even if they keep getting rejected. It's a numbers game.

Seriously, if there is one secret to being a successful writer, it is that you need to *write*. It helps you to both improve your craft and win the numbers game. Seems simple, but few writers get it.

Keeping Track: What, Where, When?

If you follow that advice—writing more stories and sending them out—you will quickly need a reliable process and/or system to keep track of your submissions, rejections, and sales. Yes, you will have sales, plural.

At a minimum, you need to track the following for each of your stories:

- *Market where story is currently submitted:* Obvious, yes, but as you begin to have more stories circulating, this becomes harder to track. Aside from knowing Story X is at Market A (and therefore can't be submitted elsewhere), you also need to know you can't submit another story to Market A until they respond to Story X.

- *Date of submission:* This lets you send the editor at Market A a *polite* query if you haven't heard back in a reasonable time on Story X. What's reasonable? I deal with that later in this chapter. Also, for income tax purposes, you must be able to show you are actively pursuing income from writing, which means being able produce a list of annual submissions.

- *Markets that have already rejected this story:* When Market A rejects Story X, you want to know where you can send it next, which can't be to a market that's already bounced the story.

- *Date of rejection from each market:* Again, you need this to support income tax claims. My system also uses this to calculate the average response time for markets where I've submitted, so I know when to query about a submission if they are on average much faster or slower than three months.

- *Market(s) that bought this story:* Yes, you will eventually sell your story. I pluralize markets because, in Section Four, you'll learn how to sell reprints and other rights and will need to track multiple markets where a story has appeared.

- *Date of story sale:* You'll want this for income tax and to track the progress of your career, etc.. And besides, it's the most enjoyable entry to make.

71

- *Date of publication:* This date is critical as it determines the year of eligibility for awards for this story.

- *Date and amount of payment:* Do I need to explain this? You'll need this for income tax, as you will likely adopt a cash (versus an accrual) method for reporting income from writing. You also want to track this to ensure the market has paid you.

That's the bare minimum. I keep track of other information for a *sale*: contributor copies due and received, country and language (and currency) of the sale (we'll cover selling translations in Chapter Twenty-one), rights sold (first, second, audio, etc.), word length of story, and more. I also track things like submissions, sales (numbers and dollars), and rejections in total and per year, as well as languages and countries in which I've been published.

But if you don't at least track the bulleted information above and have it clearly organized, readily available, and easily updated, you will get into trouble, with editors and the tax collector.

Submission Tracking Tools

So what should you use? I use a big (by now, a *very* big) spreadsheet, with my stories across as columns and the various markets down the page in rows. I organize the markets into categories: pro magazines, pro anthos, reprints, foreign markets. When I submit a story, I enter the mailing date in the corresponding cell with an "M" prefix to denote a mailing. Rejections get an "R" code, sales an "S" code, along with the date. A collection of macros give me all the reporting and summaries I need. And, no, I won't make it available to you. It's far too customized to how I sell and track.

While a spreadsheet works for me, you may want to look at the submission tracker options listed below. *A caveat:* I haven't used any of these, so I have no idea of their functionality or value. Check their features against the list I provided above.

In Chapter Seven, I discussed online market lists, including the subscription-based *Duotrope*. It's not my preferred market list, especially now that you need to pay for it, but many writers have found their submission tracker to be useful. You can sign up for a free trial if you want to check it out: duotrope.com.

Another market list site that includes a submission tracker is *The Grinder*, which has the additional benefit of being (currently) free: http://thegrinder.diabolicalplots.com.

Finally, *Sonar3* is free submission tracking software, made by Space-jock Software (Simon Haynes, Australian author of the Hal Spacejock novel series): www.spacejock.com/Sonar3.html.

How Long to Wait: Submission Queries

Earlier, I mentioned tracking the submission dates for your stories so you can send a polite query once a reasonable time has elapsed. For me and most editors, reasonable is at least four months—one month past the average response time for most pro markets.

Your query email (or letter—sigh—for the snail mail markets) should be short, polite, and to the point:

> Dear <editor name>: I submitted my story "Possums from Hell" to <market name> on <submission date>. I would appreciate an update on the status of this submission.

> Thank you for your attention.

Next, the other side of this equation: what's happening to your submitted story while you're waiting for a response and writing more stories. Let's look at how editors make decisions concerning the stories we send them.

CHAPTER 11.

BEHIND THE CURTAIN:

How an Editor Chooses (or Rejects) a Story

IN CHAPTER TEN, we discussed what to do after you send your story out to a market (reminder: write more stories and send those out, too). In this chapter, we'll look at what happens when your story arrives at your selected market and how (and why) an editor makes a decision on a story.

The Three Types of Submissions

Most markets, whether they are a magazine or an anthology, have three different submission piles. These used to be physical piles of printed manuscripts, but for most markets today, the piles will be their electronic equivalent.

The first is a very tiny pile: manuscripts from "name" authors from whom the editor might have solicited a story. These "solicits" will generally be reviewed by the Editor-in-Chief or the editorial board if one exists. Unless these stories are truly terrible, they will get published, because a big name on the cover helps sell any publication.

The second pile will be larger: unsolicited stories from authors with *professional* credits, credits which show their writing is at a level above the norm and are likely to have submitted a story that is, at a minimum, publishable.

Everything else, including all stories from beginners with no professional credits, ends up in the third pile, which is also the largest: the slush pile.

Note that I'm generalizing here. Some markets will combine my first two types of submissions above into a single pile. Others will throw my second submission type into the slush pile as well. Still others might only have one pile, including stories from big names, writers with pro credits, and beginners together in one big slush pile.

However, for you as a beginning or non-name writer, the key is to understand how the slush pile works in any market—because that's where your story will end up.

The Slush Pile

Slush is where your story goes if you have insufficient professional credits to be considered anything other than a new writer. This is why I told you in Chapter Eight to only include sales to top professional markets in your cover letter. And why I told you in Chapter Five to only submit to professional markets. Sales to non-pro markets do you absolutely no good: you'll still end up in slush.

(In case you're wondering where the term "slush pile" originated, my favorite but perhaps apocryphal version is as follows: In the early days of short fiction magazines, manuscripts were "submitted" by tossing them over the transom of the magazine's office door after hours, resulting in manuscripts piled inside the door, which would end up (in winter) covered in slush from the boots of staff as they came into the office the next morning.)

So, beginning writer, your story is now sitting in the slush pile with ever so many other manuscripts from other unknown writers. How many other stories? A top professional market or anthology typically has five hundred to a thousand submissions to consider for a *single* issue or anthology. A themed anthology might have a slightly lower range, depending on how tight their theme is, but they'll still be dealing with hundreds of submissions.

The key point for you to understand is that your little story will always be competing with hundreds and hundreds of other tales.

How Editors Read Slush

Kristine Kathryn Rusch and Dean Wesley Smith run a series of workshops on the Oregon coast for professional writers (which I highly recommend). Several of these include an interesting short fiction exercise. All attendees submit three finished but unsold short stories, which form a slush pile for the workshop. In this exercise, each participant gets to play editor by using this slush pile to assemble their own themed anthology.

Sounds easy? There's another wrinkle. You are given a very limited time to read the slush pile, like at a real editor's office. You soon learn an editor does not have time to read every word of every story in slush, which is the key educational point of the exercise.

The exercise also teaches you how to read like an editor. When an editor (or more likely, a slush reader) is reading slush, if a story doesn't engage them quickly, *in the first paragraph or at most on the first page*, they toss it aside and go on to the next one in the pile.

"What!!?!?" (I hear you cry.) "They don't read every precious word of my wonderful story, a story I poured blood and sweat and tears into?"

Nope. They don't. Remember, your little tale is only one of hundreds and hundreds of manuscripts submitted for that issue. An editor won't read every story all the way through because they physically *do not have the time*. Or the stamina, since anyone who has ever read slush will tell you the vast majority of those stories are absolute, unadulterated crap. If you don't believe me, check out this article about the experience of being a slush reader: www.guardian.co.uk/ books/booksblog/2007/may/23/theshockingtruthaboutthes

That's the reality. So how can you, as a writer, deal with that reality?

Read like an Editor

You need to learn to critique your own fiction by reading it the way an editor reads.

Back to that Kris and Dean workshop exercise. The stories submitted for the workshop anthology exercise also get critiqued in a group forum. Now, the critiquing approach in most writer groups has members give detailed feedback on a story, describing what they liked and what they didn't, sometimes providing suggestions for fixes, and maybe spending five to ten minutes giving that feedback.

Kris and Dean use a different approach. As a story comes up for discussion, each person around the room, in only five to ten *seconds*, provides a single piece of feedback: *where they stopped reading*. Typical feedback on a story sounds like this:

- "I stopped reading after the first paragraph."
- "I read to the end of the first page."
- "I read to page twelve and stopped."
- "I read all the way through, loved it, and I want to buy it for my anthology."
- "I read all the way through, but I won't be buying it."
- etc.

Kris, who was an award-winning editor at *The Magazine of Fantasy and Science Fiction* before turning to writing full-time, says she used a "three strikes and out" approach when reading submissions. Any time a story kicked her out of the reading experience, she'd make a mark in the margin. Three marks—three strikes—and she'd move on to the next story. Things that might kick an editor out of your story could be anything from a boring opening to bad grammar to not maintaining the editor's interest.

The above exercise teaches you to read your own stories the way a professional editor will, so you learn to recognize where your stories are weak. If you're in a writing critique group, try adding this type of critiquing to your process. I guarantee you'll all start selling your stories sooner.

If most readers in this type of critique tell you they stopped reading your story on the first page, you have a problem (probably several) with your opening. You can't argue with that feedback. You're outnumbered. Your opening sucks. Fix it.

If they all tell you they stopped about halfway through, then your opening engaged them, but you couldn't hold their interest. That might signal a problem with pacing, plotting, character development, or something else, but at least you know where to focus. And again, they're right, you're wrong. Go fix it.

And if most say they read your story all the way through, but they wouldn't buy it if they were an editor, you might have a problem with your ending. But more likely, your story suffers from the most common reason that stories by beginning writers are rejected—it was good but not good enough to stand out.

Why Good Stories Get Rejected: Just Not Good Enough

"What!?!?!" I hear you say again (I have good ears). "I thought only bad stories get rejected."

Nope. Although the vast majority of slush stories are truly terrible, editors frequently complain they find well-written stories that are perfectly adequate but simply aren't good *enough*. They don't rise above the rest. There's nothing *special* about them.

And when you're competing against hundreds and hundreds of other stories, you have a choice: stand out from the crowd—or stay buried in it.

This book isn't about the craft of fiction, but I'll offer one piece of advice on the creative side:

Take chances.

Editors often comment that these "good but not good enough" stories seem to be playing it safe. They make the obvious choices in plot turns and characters and themes and styles. By doing so, they end up being like most of the other "good but not good enough" stories that are readable but still rejected.

Write the story you want to write, the way you want to write it. Don't worry about what people will think of it. Don't worry about what you think the market is looking for.

In short, take chances. You're not performing open heart surgery, driving a racecar, or cliff diving. If you take a chance and fail, no one is going to die. At worst, you'll learn something about your craft. At best, you'll sell a special and unique story—the one only *you* can write.

Why Good Stories Get Rejected: Editorial Need

The other common reason good (even very good) stories are rejected is that they don't fit the editor's needs *for that particular issue or anthology.*

Your story might be an utterly awesome attack-of-the-zombie-possums story, but the editor has already bought one and can't see publishing two in the same issue. Or a big name submitted a story similar to yours (and guess which one she's buying?). Or she's full up on urban fantasy for this issue. Or she's planning a fairly dark issue, and your story is too upbeat and humorous. Or she wants an upbeat issue, and your story is a downer. In other words, it's about a "fit" the editor is looking for, and your story—no matter how awesome—just doesn't fit.

So why don't they keep your story for an upcoming issue? Many magazines used to keep a two-year inventory of stories, but most can't afford to do so anymore. Now, if they keep an inventory at all, it will be one of specific future *issues* (not general stories) and for at most five months.

The editor might explain all this to you in the rejection note, but most likely they won't tell you anything except they won't be taking your story.

Which is a perfect lead-in to our next chapter.

CHAPTER 12.
OH GOD, THEY HATE ME:
Dealing with Rejections

So NOW YOU know how editors decide to select or reject a story. Next, let's discuss how to handle an editor's most likely decision on your submitted story: a rejection.

Here's my advice for handling rejections...

Get Used to It

It sounds cruel, but my first piece of advice is to get used to rejections. If you seriously pursue a writing career, you're going to get rejections. A lot of them. Many, many more rejections than acceptances. If you can't learn to handle rejections—even *expect* rejections (yes, writers are sick puppies)—give up now.

If you think about it, the ubiquitous nature of rejections for a writer has an upside. Every writer gets them. Once you realize that, you won't feel as if you are being singled out. You aren't...it happens to all of us.

"But *why* didn't they like it?"

In the *vast* majority of cases, the editor will *not* explain *why* they rejected your story. A typical rejection letter goes something like this: "Thank you for your interest in *Awesome Possum*. Unfortunately, your story does not meet our needs at this time."

That's it. Nothing about your story. Nothing about what worked or what didn't. Zippo. Rarely, you may get specific feedback, but don't expect it. More on that later.

It's Not Personal

So an editor has now crushed your dreams without even telling you why. How do you deal with that?

First, understand they didn't reject *you*—they rejected *your story*. An editor rejects a manuscript, not a writer. In Chapter Eleven, I explained an editor rejects stories for many reasons. Yes, maybe your story was truly awful. Or maybe it was pretty good, but just didn't stand out. Or maybe it was *very* good, but didn't fit that editor's needs for that issue or anthology—the writing equivalent of the "it's not you, it's me" romantic rejection.

Here is the only thing a rejection tells you:

> *This* particular *story wasn't right for this* particular *editor at this* particular *time.*

Don't read more into a rejection beyond that.

How to Handle Rejections: A Schizophrenic Approach

So all you know is that your rejected story lies somewhere between "horrible" and "great but not a fit." Helpful, right? Yeah, not so much.

That situation is not new to a beginning writer—or to any writer. When writing a story, a writer swings between these same two extremes. At one end, we're filled with an arrogant confidence we're writing a masterpiece. At the other end, our inner critic tells us this story is crap and is going to need a complete rewrite. We constantly cycle in our mind between the Arrogant and the Fearful Beginner.

The truth generally lies somewhere in between.

But when your story is rejected, you don't know where along that spectrum it falls. So when dealing with rejections, you need to follow two paths at once—the confident "masterpiece" path and the inner critic "crap" path. Once again, you need to find the right balance between the Arrogant and the Fearful.

Keep It in the Mail

The best response to any rejection is simple:

Keep your story in the mail (or email).

In Chapters Five through Seven, I walked you through how to create your own list of top markets. Use that list. Send your story to the next market on your list, and do it *right away*.

Seriously, right away. Here's what should happen. You get the rejection. You shrug. It's a rejection. You expected that. Check your market list and submission tracker. Find your next best market that doesn't currently have a submission from you and for which this story is a fit. Compose your cover email. Attach your manuscript (or however they want you to submit). Hit "send." You're done. In ten minutes, you've dealt with a rejection in the best way possible.

Remember, it's a numbers game. The writer with the most stories in circulation wins.

What if your story is at the bad end of the spectrum? What if it truly sucks and no editor in their right mind would ever buy it?

That *is* a possibility, especially for your early efforts. But you are the worst judge of your own work (see Chapter Five), so you can't tell. Your story might be great and just hasn't found the right editor yet. So the advice is still the same.

Keep it in the mail!

Keep Learning Your Craft

But, yes, your story might truly suck. Remember writing is a craft—your chosen craft—and like any craft, you can always improve, and you will never ever completely master it. And if you're a beginner, you have more room for improvement than other writers who've been working on their craft longer than you.

So after you've submitted your rejected story to another market, work on your craft. Reread your favorite how-to book, or find another one. Do writing exercises. Whatever works to help you improve.

But most importantly, write the next story. Writers write. The only way to improve your writing is to write, so...

Keep writing!

Dealing with Editor Feedback: The Positive

On a rare occasion, an editor will actually provide you with feedback in their rejection note. Great, right?

Maybe.

Let me first say this. If an editor says nice things about your story, they mean it! If they say they would like to see more from you, *they really mean it!*

Many beginners think editors are just being polite when this happens. Go back and read Chapter Eleven. Editors are busy people. Very busy. If they took the time to write you an encouraging note on a rejection letter, *they mean it.* Bask in that glow—and send them another story right away. And move that market up to the top of your list.

Dealing with Editor Feedback: The Negative

Even more rarely, an editor might provide critical feedback on your story. Most editors will *not*. Why? First and again, they simply don't have the time. Remember an editor receives hundreds and hundreds of submissions for a *single* issue or anthology.

Second, all editors can recite horror stories of abusive replies from outraged authors verbally eviscerating them for having the temerity to criticize that writer's perfect (in the writer's mind) tale or prose.

So here's another key piece of advice:

> *Never reply to a rejection note. Ever.*

Period. End of discussion. A nice "thank you for your kind feedback" email won't hurt, but busy editors likely won't read it or remember you for sending it. But don't *ever* argue with an editor, telling them why they're wrong. They aren't. It's their opinion, whether you agree with it or not.

And they *will* remember you if you argue with them, and not in a good way.

Dealing with Editor Feedback: To Change or Not to Change

If the editor *does* comment on what worked or didn't work for them in your story, whatever you do, *do* not *revise your story* to address that feedback.

Huh? (you say) What? Why not?

Because that editor is just one person. Their feedback is just one opinion. It's too small a sample. I'll give you an example from my very first story, "Spirit Dance," for which I received the following two early rejections from two different editors:

> Editor #1: "A nice effort but a bit too slow going at the start for our tastes."

> Editor #2: "Opens well, but doesn't quite hold up to my expectations. Otherwise a solid effort."

So exactly what change should I have made to "Spirit Dance" based on that feedback? One didn't like the opening, but liked it after that. The other liked the opening but not the rest. Two diametrically opposed opinions. Their feedback also reminds us these are *personal* viewpoints—check out their use of the phrases "for our tastes" and "my expectations."

So what did I change in "Spirit Dance" when I received these rejections? Simple—nothing.

I changed nothing. The story didn't work for those editors for completely different reasons. I kept it in the mail. It sold after eight rejections to a professional anthology, giving me my first sale as a writer. That story, *in its original form*, the form those two editors rejected, has sold thirty-two times, appeared in eighteen languages, inspired a novel, and won the Aurora Award.

Keep it in the mail.

A Caveat to the Above

If you accumulate *several* pieces of feedback from editors (at *least* a half dozen) on a story that *all* cite the *same* specific problem, fix that problem. This is similar to the critique circle situation. Your story is broken in that area, so fix it.

But don't ever revise a story based on an editor's feedback and resubmit it unless they *explicitly invite* you to resubmit a revised version. We call this "revising *on spec*," and we'll discuss this situation next.

"On Spec" Rewrites

You might receive a rejection letter from an editor that says although they liked your story, it had several problems that ultimately prompted a rejection. Such markets *might* offer to reconsider the story if you're willing to revise it to address the identified problems and resubmit it.

This is called revising *on spec,* as in speculation, because you, the writer, are speculating. You are taking the chance that you may invest time and effort trying to make the requested fixes but still end up with a rejection from that market on your revised version.

So should you revise a story on spec? Well, it depends. I'll tell you what I look for before I decide to take an editor up on their on spec offer.

First, in case this isn't obvious, the editor *explicitly* has to offer to reconsider the story with revisions. Do *not* make this assumption. If an editor simply lists aspects of your story that prompted a rejection, but does not invite you to resubmit a new version, then they do *not* want to see the story again. If they want a resubmission, their letter will be completely clear on that point.

Second, it should be a professional market making the offer. I've mentioned earlier that I've sold several stories to *Cicada*, a market in the US that pays twenty-five cents a word and takes longer stories. All of my sales to that magazine have been over $1,000. When they've offered me a second chance on a story, I've taken it. The potential payback is worth the risk.

Third, if I've dealt with the editor before or know them, or if they've bought my stories in the past, my level of trust goes up, and I'm more likely to invest in the on spec revision.

Fourth, the editor needs to be very clear on exactly what they want fixed. One on spec offer I received from *Cicada* included a two-page, single spaced letter detailing their issues with the story. I knew precisely what they didn't like and what I needed to fix.

Fifth, you should agree with the weaknesses pointed out in the story. I have to believe my story will both be stronger *and* will remain the story I want to tell after I make the changes required. What if an editor asks you to fix X, Y, and Z, and you agree with X and Y, but not Z? I suggest that you make the changes for X and Y, and send the story back, explaining what you did and thanking the editor for their time. You have nothing to lose.

Sixth, and related to the last point, you need to have a plan in mind to fix your story without breaking it. On spec rewrites are never minor—they generally relate to what is called a content or substantive edit (see Chapter 15). You won't be simply tweaking prose or fixing grammar. You'll likely be dealing with major issues like characterization or the opening or the ending or a plot line. The possibility of making your story worse is real.

Finally, if an editor requests an on spec rewrite:

Do not workshop your revised version.

Editors regularly complain about writers who revise the *whole* story according to feedback from their critique group, when the editor only wanted one major thing changed. If you do this to an editor, you've wasted their time and shown you can't follow editorial direction. The editor will reject your rewrite and mentally mark you as someone they will not buy from. You will have taken an opportunity for a sale and turned it into a huge permanent negative.

Following these guidelines will not guarantee that an on spec revision and resubmission will result in a sale, but it will improve your chances.

Stay Positive

Rejections can be depressing. Sometimes it's hard for a new writer (or any writer) to remain enthusiastic about their writing dream. So how can you stay positive?

I can give my short fiction credentials in two ways:

Option 1: I have published a novel and three collections, have over a hundred and fifty story sales in twenty-five languages and thirty countries, three award wins, two dozen award short-lists, and over a million words of fiction sold.

Option 2: I've been rejected over eight hundred times.

Guess which version I use when I'm presenting myself to editors or tell myself when I get rejections?

But understand this: those two versions of my credentials are two sides of the same coin. I wouldn't have those books and sales and awards if I hadn't made almost a thousand submissions—submissions that also drove those rejections.

You can't separate success from rejection.

Keep writing stories. And keep them in the mail.

CHAPTER 13.
DRAWING THE LINE:
When to Stop Submitting a Story

In Chapter Twelve, we dealt with handling rejections. In this chapter, we'll look at one of the most common questions in selling short fiction: how many rejections on a story are too many?

Never Give Up—Never Surrender

In other words, is there a point where you should decide a story is never going to sell? Is there a magic rejection count that signals a story should go on the shelf? And the answer is...

No.

As you learned in the previous chapter, the best way to deal with rejections is to keep the story in the mail.

But surely any story that, say, twenty different editors have bounced can't be a very good story?

Trust me, at twenty rejections, it's still a virgin. Let me give you some examples from my own experience.

Early in my career, I sold my story "The Boys Are Back in Town" to *Cicada*, an excellent young-adult magazine in the US. Up to that point, "The Boys" had collected twenty-six rejections. It became the lead story in the *Cicada* issue in which it appeared. I included it in my second collection, *Chimerascope*, and it garnered nice reviews.

I've since sold multiple times to *Cicada*. How much did *Cicada* pay me for a story that had over two dozen rejections?

Two thousand dollars. And in case you're not aware, that is a *lot* of money for a short story. Good thing I didn't quit on that story, right?

Here are two more recent and even more telling examples. I mentioned in Chapter Twelve that the first story I ever wrote, "Spirit Dance," was also the first story I ever sold, to the Canadian anthology series *Tesseracts*. It sold after eight rejections. Eight rejections. That's not many, right?

The second and third stories I wrote, also set in my Heroka shapeshifter universe, were "A Bird in the Hand" and "Dream Flight." After "Spirit Dance" sold, I expected these stories to also sell quickly.

Nope. They didn't. I continued to write and sell stories, but "A Bird in the Hand" and "Dream Flight" remained unsold, year after year.

But I kept them both in the mail. I never gave up on them. Finally, in 2011, "A Bird in the Hand" appeared in *Warrior Wisewoman 3*, a popular anthology series. Then, in late 2013, I sold "Dream Flight" to *The Dark Magazine*, a new pro magazine, where it appeared as the lead story in their third issue.

Those two sales came *fifteen and seventeen years* respectively after I wrote the stories and after (wait for it) *sixty-five and sixty-four* rejections respectively.

So how long is too long? Never. How many rejections are too many? No such number.

Never give up on a story. Keep it in the mail.

Revisiting a Story That Keeps Going Bouncy-Bouncy

In the previous chapter, I recommended not changing a story based on a few feedback comments on rejection letters. So, did I leave "A

Bird in the Hand" and "Dream Flight" unchanged through those sixty-plus rejections?

No, I revisited the stories, maybe twice, over those years, but *not* to address feedback from editors in their rejection letters.

Rather, I reread those stories with fresh eyes and with the deeper knowledge of my craft I'd acquired since I wrote them as a complete beginner. And yes, I made changes to the original versions. But nothing major. Smoother prose, better dialog, fewer speech attributions. Nothing more than tweaks.

Because the stories themselves still stood up, in my biased view. Most importantly, *they were still the stories I wanted to tell*. And I still believed they would sell.

So I kept them in the mail. (Yes, you're right—I'm repeating that a lot. It must be important.)

What to Do When You Run Out of Markets

In Chapter Seven, we talked about selecting the best markets for your stories. You also learned to submit only to markets that pay professional rates or have high prestige in the industry. Most importantly, you learned to *start at the top* of that list and work your way down with each rejection until you sell the story.

So what happens when you reach the bottom of your list? What should you do when you've run out of professional markets?

The most important thing is to never lower your standards. Do *not* submit that story to markets below your minimum threshold.

Instead, you need to be patient. You need to wait for new professional markets to emerge. And they will.

When I was receiving my constant stream of rejections on "A Bird in the Hand" and "Dream Flight," my target list held far less than the sixty-plus markets that rejected those stories before they sold. I ran out of markets quickly for those stories. So what did I do?

I waited. I was patient. I checked Ralan's market list (www.ralan. com) regularly and stayed current on new markets. I also kept track of when editors changed at the professional magazines on my target list, and resubmitted there. Mostly, I waited for new anthologies.

Your best chance for finding new markets will always be anthologies. New magazines, especially those paying professional rates, don't come along very often (although the rise of online and ebook magazines is starting to change that).

But every year brings a new batch of professional anthologies, and the best part about anthologies, especially for a hard-to-sell story, is that they are usually *themed*. I eventually sold "A Bird in the Hand" to *Warrior Wisewoman*, an anthology series with a theme of strong woman protagonists in science fiction, a great fit for my story of a kick-ass female shapeshifter captured in a secret government laboratory.

It's a Numbers Game

Yes, I'm repeating that a lot, too—because it is *critical* to your career success. While "A Bird in the Hand" and "Dream Flight" were racking up rejections, I was racking up sales, awards and recognition, because *I kept writing other stories and sending them out.*

In those seventeen years, I had over a hundred sales, won three awards, and made the final ballot for two dozen other awards, including the John W. Campbell for Best New Writer. If I hadn't kept writing, I wouldn't have accomplished any of that. I also would never have been able to stand up to the constant ego pummeling of the rejections.

"A Bird in the Hand" and "Dream Flight" were just two more stories of mine making the rounds. I was getting lots of positive reinforcement about my writing from other stories that were selling and attracting award notice, so it was easy to continue to still believe in stories that hadn't sold.

So...

Keep writing stories.

Keep them in the mail.

Never give up on a story.

~~~

This chapter finishes Section Two on how to *market* your short fiction, which has focused on helping you to actually sell a story.

Next, in Section Three, we move on to the happier topic of what happens when you *do* sell a story.

SECTION III

YOU'VE SOLD A STORY:

CONTRACTS, EDITING, AND REALITY

In Section Two, we learned everything you need to know about correctly submitting your stories to the right markets, dealing with rejections, and keeping your stories in the mail. Everything in the last section was aimed at getting you to the point where you sold your first story.

Well, congratulations! You've sold a story! We can now deal with the happier process of everything that happens and that you need to know after you've made a story sale.

Here we will cover short fiction contracts, working with editors and copy-editors, dealing with reviews, what to expect on your future submissions after you've sold your first story.

Let's get started.

CHAPTER 14.

SIGN HERE:

What to Look (Out) for in Short Fiction Contracts

YOU CLICK ON an email from that great pro magazine you've been trying to sell to for so long. What!? They love your story! They want to buy it! You're going to be a professionally published author!

Awesome! Seriously, congratulations!

Take a moment to enjoy that feeling of accomplishment and to bask in the warm glow of success. Very few people reach this point. Good for you. Bask, bask, bask...

Okay, enough with the basking. Time to get to work.

Yeah, sorry to tell you, but your work doesn't end when you sell a story. You just start a new series of tasks, beginning with confronting your first short fiction contract and your next chance to make a serious mistake. This chapter will help you avoid that.

Some Caveats

This topic would require an entire college course to cover, so I'll only be hitting the highlights. And to again quote the multi-award winning, multi-genre writer, Kristine Kathryn Rusch: I am not a lawyer, nor do I play one on TV.

I'll give advice here on short fiction contracts, but I can't be held responsible for anything you sign. Your career. Your decision. You need to learn the industry in which you've decided to build a career. That means learning to understand short fiction contracts.

Keeping Your Stories as Yours

Contracts are incredibly important. Many writers don't get that. Contracts determine who controls the rights to *your* stories. Signing a bad contract can mean your stories aren't yours anymore. Other bad things can happen, but giving up more rights than you should for longer than you should sits at the top of the list.

Kris Rusch has another line I like to quote: "There are only two things a writer can control—the stories they write and the contracts they sign."

So, yeah...contracts are important.

The Contract as a Starting Point

When you receive your contract, remember one thing: it's just a document. Think of it as a story draft that may still need editing. It is not carved in stone. It can be changed.

But the publisher won't change your contract if *you* don't review it for what needs to be changed—and if *you* don't request those changes.

Think of a contract from a publisher as a suggested starting point in a discussion. A business-like and professional discussion, but still a discussion, one in which you request changes you want to see.

I'm not trying to turn you into a high-powered negotiator. You don't need to be. You just need to do the following:

- Be informed about the key clauses to look for in a short fiction contract (we review these below);

- Know what terms you'll bend on and what you won't (your career, your decision); and,

- Don't be too afraid (or too timid / polite / stupid) to request changes in the contract.

(By the way, although mostly aimed at the much more complex book contract situation, Kris Rusch has an excellent series of posts on negotiation in her acclaimed "A Freelancer Survival Guide" blog series (kriswrites.com/freelancers-survival-guide-table-of-contents/), which is now available as a book as well. The negotiation posts are #37-42.)

Understanding Rights (Revisited)

Back in Chapter Three, I explained why you never actually "sell" a story, and discussed in detail the licensing of rights for your fiction.

STOP.

No, seriously, stop. If you *haven't* read Chapter Three, go back and read it *now*. In fact, even if you *have* read it, go back and reread it now.

That is the most important chapter in this book. If you don't understand licensing of rights for fiction, you are going to have a very, very unhappy career, if you manage to have a career at all. Plus, none of what we talk about below will make any sense.

So go. Read Chapter Three now. I'll wait.

The Key Things to Look for in Short Fiction Contracts

Ok, you're back and hopefully better educated or refreshed on licensing and rights. Let's talk contracts.

Short fiction contracts are generally straight-forward, but still contain things to look out for because the standard contract from a publisher generally favors the publisher (surprise, surprise).

Here are the key things I focus on in any short story contract:

1. What rights are being requested?
2. When do those rights revert to me?
3. What legal liability am I being asked to accept?
4. What happens if the story is never published?
5. What happens if this market folds or is sold?
6. Will there be a published declaration of my copyright?
7. What control will I have over changes to my story?
8. What am I being paid for these rights?

Let's go through each of these in detail, or as much detail as I can cover in a book not intended as a law course text.

Key Thing #1. What Rights Are Being Requested?

I won't repeat what is in Chapter Three (because you just reread it, right?). You need to look at the specific rights the market is requesting and decide if those are reasonable and fair requests. You then need to decide if you're willing to give up those rights to get this sale.

For example, if a magazine is currently print only, but is asking for audio rights because they may at an undefined point in the future want to publish an audio book version, you need to decide if that is reasonable. Your career, your decision.

Let's discuss some specific common situations that you should be alert for.

Electronic vs. Audio: Most markets will request Electronic Rights if they will be including your story in an ebook or online edition. However, technically, an audio book is also an electronic form of presentation. For this reason, I explicitly exclude audio rights from electronic rights granted if the contract has not already done so (unless of course if the market also produces an audio edition).

Geography and Electronic Rights: Related to this, if the market requests Electronic Rights, they are automatically requesting World Rights.

They may explicitly state that, but if they don't, just understand that if you grant Electronic Rights, you are granting World Rights.

World Rights and Language: If a market requests World Rights without stating a particular language, do not assume that you are granting World Rights only in the language of the contract. Always add a clause that explicitly states the applicable language (e.g., World Rights in English).

Online Archiving Rights: If you sell to an online magazine, they may request the rights to maintain your story in an online archive, even after the original rights revert to you. In the past, I would always request this clause to be removed. First, such magazines generally don't offer any additional fees for this right. Second, many markets will not be interested in purchasing reprint rights for my story if it's freely available online.

However, with the sharp rise in online markets, this request is becoming more common. Most of these markets keep their back issues available online. If you refuse archiving for your story, the editor would be unable to archive the entire issue or anthology containing your story. So they'd likely end up rejecting your story, and you'd lose a sale.

Also, sometimes editors will purchase reprint rights even if the story is available online. For example, they may be publishing an anthology or themed issue for which the story is a perfect fit. And sometimes, both the archival market and the new market may benefit, especially if the story is from a well-known author, reinforcing the prestige of both markets. Finally, different publications have different audiences. A story that ran online can find an entirely new audience by appearing in a print publication.

So my current advice is to leave the archiving rights clause in, *as long as your story will remain as part of the original issue or anthology* in its archived form. I would advise against granting archiving rights for a standalone version of your story. But it's your career, so it's your decision.

Anthology Rights for a Magazine Market: You might encounter a request from a magazine publisher for anthology rights. I've sold several stories to *Cicada*, the US young adult magazine that pays twenty-five cents a word, a fantastic rate for genre fiction. Their contract requested non-exclusive rights to republish the story in an anthology (likely a "best of" volume). They offered 50% of the original fee (twelve and a half cents a word) or a 50% split of fees they received if a third party published the anthology.

I signed all of their contracts containing that clause. First, the pay rate was better than you'll find for any reprint market (and better than most professional markets for first rights sales). Second, they asked for non-exclusive rights. Granting them those rights did not restrict me from reselling the story as a reprint to another market, once the first rights reverted to me—a great segue to question #2.

Key Thing #2. When Do These Rights Revert to Me after Publication?

Next, you need to check when the rights you're licensing revert to you. That is, when can you license those rights again to another publisher or exercise those rights yourself in any other way such as indie publishing.

As discussed in Chapter Three, for a magazine contract, rights typically revert to you after a specified period following the publication of the issue containing your story, a period which usually matches or slightly overlaps when their next issue appears. This is only fair—they don't want your story appearing in a competing market as a reprint until they've had a chance to sell their issue with the same story.

For anthologies, a one-year post-publication reversion clause is typical. Book publishing has higher costs and so requires a longer period to get their investment back, compared to magazines, which also have an existing subscriber base.

All you need to do here is to ensure (a) a clear reversion clause is included, and (b) the reversion period is in line with the above guidance.

Key Thing #3. What Legal Liability Am I Being Asked to Accept?

Every contract will have a clause, intended to protect the publisher, asking the author to warrant they are the sole author of this story, they haven't plagiarized any of it, it does not contravene any laws, etc.. With this clause, the publisher is asking you to declare that nothing about this story is going to prompt a lawsuit against them.

That's fair. But ensure any such clause includes the italicized part in the following example, which is an amalgam from contracts I've signed (the italics are mine):

> "You, the Author, warrants that the Work is original; that you are its sole creator and owner; that you have full power to make this agreement; that neither the Work nor any part of it is in the public domain; that neither the Work nor any part of it infringes on another's copyright; and that the Work does not invade anyone's right of privacy nor is contrary to law. You agree to indemnify and hold harmless the Publisher from any and all costs and expenses (including reasonable legal fees) arising from any claims, suits, judgments or settlements resulting from a breach of the above warranties *that are sustained in a court of law*."

The italicized part protects you from having to cover the publisher's legal fees and expenses required to defend nuisance suits brought against that publisher and you by your bitter ex-spouse or a random nut job who is convinced you stole their story idea of possum shape-shifters. Without the underlined wording, even if those suits are thrown out of court, you'll still be on the hook for covering costs up to that point and likely would remain out-of-pocket for some of the costs. With the underlined part, you'll be liable for claims upheld against you in court—that is, you'll only pay for situations where you are proven to be in the wrong.

Key Thing #4. What Happens If the Story Is Never Published?

This is another form of the issue of reversion of rights. If the contract's reversion clause is based solely on the assumed publication date of the magazine issue or the anthology containing your story, then what happens if that market *never* publishes your story? What if they just decide to hold onto it for a while? And then a while longer? And longer?

If you signed a contract that didn't cover this situation, then you're stuck. The publisher legally holds the rights to your story, and there those rights will sit.

So you need to include a clause specifying a strict time limit on when rights revert to you *regardless of whether the story is published*. I generally suggest something like one year after the date of the signing of the contract for a magazine, or two years for an anthology.

You can pick any time period you're comfortable with, but be reasonable. For most magazines, a year is reasonable; less than a year not so much. Some magazines buy well in advance of expected publication. For my twenty-five cent per word market I mentioned above, I'd be fine with giving them two years, since they pay so well.

The other issue to deal with in this situation is payment. Most markets that include this type of reversion clause will also agree to pay the author even if they don't publish their story. They've tied up the rights for that story for all that time, so the author deserves to be compensated for not being able to market the story elsewhere. If your contract does not address the issue of payment on delayed or non-publication, then you should add that as well.

Putting this all together, you should look for (and suggest if absent) a clause something along the lines of the following:

> "If the Story remains unpublished one year after the date of signing of this agreement, then all rights granted under

paragraph xx above shall revert to the Author, and the Author shall remain entitled to all payments due under paragraph yy."

Or alternatively:

"If the Story remains unpublished one year after the date of signing of this agreement, then all rights granted under paragraph xx above shall revert to the Author, and the Author shall be entitled to retain all payments received to that date."

Key Thing #5. What Happens If the Market Folds or Is Sold?

A contract should also specify what happens to your rights should this market suddenly cease to exist. The easiest way is to include a clause that states something such as:

"In the event that [magazine name] ceases to publish (or the publication of [anthology name] is canceled), then all rights granted under paragraph xx above shall immediately revert to the Author."

You can also include one of the above clauses about still getting paid, but if they're folding, good luck on collecting.

The contract should also address what happens to your rights when the market or publisher that bought your story is purchased by another publisher. The safest option is to include a clause something along the lines of:

"No assignment of this contract or the rights granted herein shall be binding without the written consent of the Author."

That way, the original publisher cannot assign your contract to the new publisher. That is, they cannot include your contract and the associated rights to your story in the assets they sell to the new owner. You get to decide if you still want to sell your story to the new kid on the block or just get the rights back. If the new publisher wants your story, they'd need to offer you a new contract.

Key Thing #6. What Control Will I Have over Changes to My Story?

I'll be covering the editing process in Chapter Fifteen, but for now just know it doesn't hurt to include something in the contract along the lines of:

> "Publisher will make no major alterations to the Work's text or title without the Author's written approval."

It's reasonable if the publisher wants to include something like:

> "The Publisher reserves the right to make minor copy-editing to the text of the Work to conform to our customary form and usage."

This latter relates to things like house style, US versus UK spelling, etc..

Key Thing #7. Will There Be a Published Declaration of My Copyright?

Look for a clause along the lines of:

> "The Author's copyright will prominently accompany the Work when published identifying the author as [Author's pen name]."

This is especially important if the name you publish under differs from the name under which you will be signing the contract. I go by "Doug" in casual correspondence, but I always publish under "Douglas." A small thing, but with my last name, I want to at least be consistent with the use of my first name when my by-line appears.

Key Thing #8. What Payment Are They Offering for These Rights?

Yes, I list payment last. It's easy to check for and is the one thing in this list that doesn't carry any on-going or post-publication down-side potential for a writer if you get it wrong in a contract.

Check the dollar amount shown against the word rate in their submission guidelines and the word count for your story. Make sure you know which word count method the market is using. See Chapter Eight for an explanation of these methods.

Also check on the promised *timing* of the payment. When will they send you your money? Most markets pay on publication, meaning at some point after the magazine issue or anthology is physically published and available for purchase. The "at some point" can vary by market, but a couple of months after publication is not unusual. Keeping track of who still owes you money is another part of a writer's life. Get used to it.

A few markets pay on acceptance, which generally means when you've signed the contract, but can also mean when you and the editor have agreed on any changes they've requested to the story.

Finally, if this is a sale to a print market, check the number of contributor copies (copies of the issue or anthology containing your story) you'll receive. You generally always receive at least one copy, sometimes two. If they only offer one, I ask for two—one for my brag shelf and one for my files. They can only say no.

Is That All There Is?

Have I covered every clause you could find in a short fiction contract? No, but I've covered the most critical ones (in my view) you should always ensure are included before you sign.

One other point: please don't ask me to review any contract or answer any questions on a contract you have in front of you. It's not my job to figure out your contracts. It's yours.

And that's a perfect setup for me to close with yet another reminder on anything you are asked to sign as a writer...

Your career. Your decision. Try to make it an informed one.

CHAPTER 15.
I LOVE YOUR STORY.
NOW CHANGE IT:
Working with an Editor

Now THAT YOU have signed a reasonable and fair contract for your story, we're ready to talk about working with an editor on getting your story ready for publication.

Don't Worry—Be Happy

If you've sold to a top market, you can expect an editor to work with you to edit your story before they publish it. This is a *good* thing for you as a writer. A professional editor can only improve your story. If you've (foolishly) sold your story to a non-pro market, you'll be lucky to get any editing done on your work at all.

So if a market, after buying your story, says you'll be receiving editing suggestions, don't worry—be happy. Remember: they loved your story enough to give you money for it. Think of editing as a free service the publisher provides to make your great story even greater and make you look even better as a writer. It's all goodness.

So What's Not to Like about My Story?

But (you say) they bought my story already. Why would they want to change it?

Um, because *every* story can always be improved. If you're the Arrogant Beginner we met in Chapter One who believes your prose is so perfect that no one should ever dare to suggest a change, you need to change your viewpoint quickly. Or be prepared for a short and unhappy career.

> *If you can't work with an editor, you will never be*
> *a professional writer.*

This is just one specific example of the broader principle that every writer needs to learn to accept constructive feedback.

This doesn't mean you must accept every editing suggestion for your story (more on that later). But you should enter into any editing discussion with a positive attitude and an understanding that the goal is to make your story better, to the benefit of both you and the publication that bought the story.

And revision suggestions from a professional market that has *bought* your story (they *want* to publish it—they *like* it!) will be as constructive as constructive can be.

Now let's review the types of edits that can occur on a short fiction manuscript.

Types of Editing: Content Editing

Content edits are at the story level, not at the word, sentence, or even paragraph level. A content edit is *substantive*. It focuses on the big stuff — plot confusion, pacing issues, story structure, poor information flow, weak characterization or character arcs, unnecessary sub-plots, unclear motivation, lack of setting detail, etc. That is, a content edit focuses on problems in your story often requiring a heavy revision of the story, if not a rewrite.

I include content editing in this chapter for the purpose of completeness on the editing topic. You're unlikely to encounter this type of edit for a short story. If your story has any of the issues listed above, it's unlikely a short fiction market will buy it. They can't take the chance you will be able to fix it to their satisfaction in time for publication.

"On Spec" Rewrites

However, you *might* encounter substantive content editing suggestions *before* you make a sale, in a rejection letter that says they liked your story but it had several problems that ultimately prompted a rejection. Such markets *might* offer to reconsider the story if you're willing to revise it to address the identified problems and resubmit it.

We dealt with this in Chapter 12. It's called revising *on spec*, as in speculation. Please reread that section if you haven't already done so, as the advice there applies to any substantive or content editing suggestions that you receive on an already accepted story.

Types of Editing: Line Editing

Line edits focus less on the story and more on the prose. This is the typical type of editing you'll receive for a short story before publication, if you're lucky. Yes, I said lucky. Remember, the editor wants to make your story stronger and make you look better as a writer.

A line edit could include suggestions for any of the following:

- Strengthening weak prose, including fixing awkward sentences, addressing weak verb forms, making better word choices, cutting unnecessary words, using stronger nouns and verbs, killing adverbs, etc.

- Varying sentence structure and improving the rhythm of the prose

- Changing paragraph breaks

- Replacing repeated words in close proximity

- Correcting grammatical and spelling errors

- Reducing use of unnecessary speech attributions

- Strengthening dialog
- Eliminating clichés
- Changing to conform to the house style
- ...and much more.

Now, hopefully, you've tried to catch all the above yourself (well, except for house style) before you submitted the story, so why do you need another edit pass? Again, because any story can always be improved. A second set of eyes, especially from a professional editor reading a story from a relative newcomer, will always find something to help strengthen the story.

And if they don't find anything to fix, no problem. It was their time spent, not yours.

Types of Editing: Copy Editing

The final type of editing that occurs on a story in a professional market is copy editing. This is a review of the final version of your story, the version that incorporates all the edits discussed above. Copy editing is a final check for the small stuff: typos, spelling, house styles, missing or repeated words, punctuation, etc..

Short fiction markets typically incorporate the copy edit into the line editing exercise, so that you, the author, will have just a single editing discussion.

Types of Editing: Page Proofs

This is an editing step that falls solely on you as the author. If you've sold to a professional market, you can expect to receive page proofs—a copy of how your story will appear in the actual publication. These are typically sent to you as a PDF attachment to an email these days.

It's your responsibility to quickly review these page proofs to catch any remaining *minor* problems that need to be fixed. I emphasize *minor*. Now is *not* the time to rewrite the ending. It's too late. The publisher's production schedule (and budget) won't be able to accommodate major changes at this stage.

Types of Editing: Suggested Reading

If you'd like to read more on the types of editing you'll encounter as a writer, but focused on novels versus short stories, then read Kris Rusch's post on editorial revisions for novelists: kriswrites. com/2013/01/23/the-business-rusch-editorial-revisions/.

Working with an Editor: The Mechanics

Above, I explained that the first edit you'll receive on a sold story will likely be a combination line and copy edit. Most editors these days work directly on an electronic version of your story with "track changes" and "show markup" turned on. I'm using MS-Word terminology here. If you use a different word processor, I'm guessing you can still figure out what I mean. They may also insert comments for a suggested change to explain why their edit makes the story or prose stronger. They'll then email you the red-lined version of the story file.

Seeing a sea of red-lining can make any writer see red emotionally as well. How dare they change your perfect prose? Well, sunshine, guess what? Your prose isn't perfect, and it probably never will be. Any second set of eyes will always improve a story.

So remember, editing will make your story better and make *you* look better as a writer. Your default position, especially as a beginner, should always be to not only accept editing suggestions, but to want them.

That being said, here's a suggested approach to help you cope with that sea of red:

- Read the suggested edits without making any decisions. Just read looking for patterns and issues the editor has found.

- Set the edited version aside for at least a day.

- Read the story again, doing a triage on suggested edits: ones that are easy to say "yes" to, ones you will not bend on (keep these to a minimum), and ones you're not sure about.

- Go through the story one more time, ensuring you're serious about each time you're saying "no" to a suggested edit — "serious" means you'd pull the story before you'd agree to those changes.

- Next, review the edits you weren't sure about, moving them to the Yes or the No category.

- Do a count of each Yes and No. If you're declining more edits than you're accepting, you're making a mistake, especially if you're a beginning writer and this is a top professional market.

- Accept the edits you agree with, and reject the others, explaining (either in the manuscript or in your cover email back to the editor) why you're saying no or offering a compromise fix.

There. You're done. Easy, right? No, probably not. Especially for your first sale. But it will get easier.

Working with an Editor: What Not to Do

I mentioned this in Chapter 12 when we discussed *on spec* rewrites, but it's worth repeating here.

Do not workshop your revised version.

Editors regularly complain about writers who revise their entire story according to feedback from their critique group, when the editor only wanted specific changes made. This happens mostly on requests for substantive edits, but the advice applies to any edit.

If you do this to an editor, you've wasted their time and shown you can't follow editorial direction. The editor will cancel your contract and add you to their list of writers they will not work with. You will have lost a sale and damaged your reputation. So don't do it.

When to Say No

So when should you say "no" to an editing suggestion? I wish I could give you an easy answer, but I can't. But I can give you some guidelines.

For any suggested edit you disagree with, the likelihood you are wrong and the editor is right varies directly with how professional the market is and inversely with your own experience. If you're dealing with one of the top professional markets, they're right and you're wrong. If you're a beginning writer, they're right and you're wrong. Deal with it. As I said earlier, if you can't work with an editor, you will never be a professional writer.

However, if you're dealing with a lower level market, the likelihood of having a less experienced editor goes up. And if you've been selling to top markets for a few years, the likelihood of you being able to separate bad editing from your personal ego also increases.

Some suggested edits are easy to reject. They change the meaning of a sentence or a passage. They aren't in the right voice or vocabulary for that point-of-view character. Other edits are less easy to dismiss.

I'll say no if a suggestion changes the rhythm of my prose. Sometimes I couldn't care less if a sentence is grammatically correct. If you're writing strong prose, your work should set off alarm bells in any grammar checker. For me, I love partial sentences. One word paragraphs. Beginning sentences with "And." And (see?) a dozen other stylistic idiosyncrasies that are grammatically incorrect but define my prose style—whatever works to make my prose *sound* the way I want it to, as well as mean what it needs to mean. If an editor tries to change the sound of my prose, I'll say no.

Does this help you? Probably not. Unfortunately, for a beginning writer, knowing when to agree to edits and when to say no is very much the same problem of recognizing in yourself the Arrogant or the Fearful Beginner. The Arrogant Beginner will rail against any and all edits. The Fearful Beginner will accept all edits, even bad ones. You need to find the middle ground.

But my general guideline holds: if you're saying *no* more than *yes* in the editing process, then you're probably wrong.

Checking Page Proofs

Page proofs (the way your story will look in the final publication) are usually sent to you as a PDF file these days. Here's the process I use to check page proofs.

I copy my most recent version of the story (incorporating any agreed edits) from my Word document into a free piece of software called ReadPlease. This program then reads my story back to me, in a wonderfully HAL-like, trying-hard-to-be-human, computerized voice, while I follow along reading the PDF page proofs.

I find this process an easy way to catch any discrepancies in the two versions. When I find a change, I simply decide if I agree with it or not. If I agree, no problem—I don't need to do anything. But if I disagree, I respond to the copy editor right away, identifying the page and line number and the change I'm requesting.

Record Keeping

If this is a first rights sale, I change my Word file copy of the manuscript to incorporate whatever edits I accepted for this publication. If I gave in on a suggested edit, I might not make that change if I still prefer my original version. But in general, I want the version of the story I might later resell as a reprint or foreign translation to match the form in which it first appeared. That first published version becomes my "master" copy for future second rights sales for that story.

Reprints

I'll be discussing selling second rights (reprints) in detail in Section Four, but I'll mention that possibility here since it presents a special case for dealing with edits. If an editor accepts your story as a reprint, in most cases, they will not suggest any major editing, except possibly to adhere to their house style. They know it's been published and likely edited before.

But not always. I've had several reprint situations where an editor has come back to me with line edits, sometimes fairly extensive. This has usually happened where the line editor was not the acquiring editor and wasn't aware the story was a reprint. But I've also had eager and inexperienced line editors think they can still improve the story.

Maybe they can, but in this case, that's not the point.

I generally reject any suggested edits to a previously published story (again, except for house style differences). I don't like having different versions of the same story out there. The only exceptions I make are where an editor catches an error or suggests a strong improvement to the prose. Otherwise, I'll decline the edit suggestion.

And yes, that can cost you a reprint sale. I once made a reprint sale of my humorous SF space opera story, "Murphy's Law," to an anthology. That story had originally appeared in *Baen's Universe*, a top paying professional market at the time. The story is also included in my collection, *Chimerascope*. In other words, it had already received two very professional edits.

The anthology editor suggested several very questionable edits, which I declined. The editor responded by dropping me from the anthology. Shrug. His loss, not mine. I'll resell that story again somewhere else, but it's going to be the version I want published and not one with broken prose.

As always, in these situations:

Your career, your decision.

CHAPTER 16.
BUT YOU BOUGHT MY LAST STORY:
What a First Sale Really Means

IN THIS CHAPTER, we'll cover what to expect the next time you submit a story after you've made your first sale, including submitting to the market that just published you.

Your First Sale! Enjoy the Warm Glow

You've sold your first story! It's been published! It's a great feeling, isn't it? Somebody actually *is* out there listening. You're not just tossing your stories into the dark abyss of oblivion. Real honest-to-goodness readers not related to you are going to read your words. Cool, eh? Plus you're getting paid real *money* for your work (you did submit to a paying market, right?).

That first sale is a major ego boost, and beginning writers always need that. It's an affirmation that you're on the right path, that you can sell what you write, that your dream is achievable.

Yes, the feeling from your first sale is awesome and will always remain with you as a warm fuzzy glow somewhere in your heart. I remember receiving my acceptance letter from *Tesseracts 6* for "Spirit Dance" in the mail (yes, the kind that shows up in an envelope in your mailbox—this was the nineties) on New Year's Eve. What better way to end one year and start another? I can still remember the thrill of reading that acceptance letter, of holding the book in my hands, of the book launch. That first story eventually led to my first award and later to my first novel, *The Wolf at the End of the World*.

So, yeah, bask in the glow. Enjoy the warm fuzzies.

And Now for Reality...

So now you've made it, right?

Wrong. You've sold a story. One story. That's it.

Your first sale doesn't guarantee you're going to sell the next story to the next market where you submit. It doesn't even guarantee the market that just published your first sale will buy the next story you send them. Or any story you ever send them again.

Surprised? Most beginners are. Most believe their first sale has launched them and now editors will snap up everything they write.

Let me tell you a story. My second sale, and my first big professional sale, was to the UK magazine, *InterZone*, back when David Pringle still owned it before it became part of the excellent TTA Press stable of magazines under Andy Cox.

This was huge to me. *InterZone* was one of my favorite magazines with a high prestige factor. People knew *InterZone*. Selling to them was a *big* deal. I figured I'd made it. I promptly moved them to the top of my market list for submissions and mailed them off my next story.

Which David rejected. As he rejected every other story I sent him. I've sold to *InterZone* since, but never again while David was editor. Obviously, I still went on to sell more stories to pro markets, but I still remember my shock at those subsequent rejections from *InterZone*. Those bounces were almost as surprising as my first acceptance.

Why One Sale Doesn't Guarantee the Next

Why does that happen? Obviously, you say, the editor likes your writing, or they wouldn't have bought your first story. So why shouldn't they buy your next one?

Because editors buy stories, not writers. Oh, sure, some markets will always buy Stephen King or Neil Gaiman or any other well-known writer everyone knows. But those editors buy those writers precisely because we know them. A "name" writer on the cover helps sell their issue or their anthology. Plus they know they're going to get a good, or at worst, a publishable story from a big name. Big payback, low risk.

If you've sold one story, you're not a name. One day, hopefully, but not yet. And, unless you're a name, you need to remember an editor buys a story not a writer. Your next story will still compete with the hundreds of other stories any market receives. If you need to refresh your memory on how an editor makes a buying decision, go back and reread Chapter Eleven.

The way to sell your *next* story is the same as how to sell your *first* story: continue to write the best stories you can, keep them in the mail, and keep learning your craft. Those are the only steps you control as a writer.

What Your First Sale Really Means

So if your first sale doesn't guarantee the next one, what *does* it mean, aside from the warm fuzzies?

Well, most importantly, you can now cite a professional publication credit in your future cover letters, which might get you out of the slush pile. Or it might not (sorry, but it's only one sale).

Even if it does get you out of the slush pile for a market, that only means someone is going to read your story earlier than the stories sitting in slush. And all *that* means is you'll get faster rejections than in the past.

You also may find you start to get more personalized rejections, although don't count on it. The markets you've sold to are more likely to start doing that for you, but no promises even there.

Faster Rejections Are a Good Thing

"What?!? That's it?" you say (or perhaps scream). "I finally sell a story, and all it brings me are *faster* rejections?"

Uh, yeah. Sorry, but that's the reality.

Why? Again, because it's just one sale. You haven't done that much in the cold cruel world of professional publishing. *You* know you have, and you can feel how huge that first sale was to you. But you are still only one of hundreds of thousands of wannabe writers building their credits like you are, one sale at a time.

And don't discount faster rejections. They mean you can get that story out to another market sooner. Remember what you learned in Chapter Ten: it's a numbers game. The writer with the most stories out in front of the most pro markets is going to win. Eventually, a story that keeps getting rejected is going to sell. Faster rejections along the way means you will sell your stories sooner.

CHAPTER 17.
THEY SAID WHAT?!?:
Dealing with Reviews

So FAR IN this section, which deals with what happens when you finally sell a story, we've covered short fiction contracts, working with an editor, and what your first sale *really* means. In this chapter, we discuss the classic good news / bad news aspect of publishing your first story—the ever anticipated, ever dreaded reviews.

What Reviews Really Are

Write this down. Put it over your writing desk. Memorize it. Burn it into your consciousness.

A review is one person's opinion.

First, a review is *opinion*, not fact. It is subjective, not objective. A review is colored by that reviewer's unique, particular, and peculiar tastes, and by their biases, experiences, prejudices, blind spots, emotional makeup, personality, religious beliefs, intellect, life view, level of medication, and whether they burned their toast the day they wrote the review.

Second, that opinion belongs to a single, solitary *individual*. The world's population is now over seven billion people. The person who reviewed your story represents 0.000000014% of humanity. One opinion in seven billion.

125

In other words, any review of your story, *good or bad*, is simply not important. To you as a writer, it means nothing.

Notice that I said good or bad. A bad review is just one person's opinion. So is a good review. So here's the next piece of advice for you to pin over your writing desk:

Don't believe your reviews.

Good or bad, a review means *nothing*. Whether a reviewer trashes your story as incoherent drivel or praises it as the greatest piece of modern fiction ever, their review remains *the opinion of a single individual*. It means nothing.

The Best Advice You Will Ever Ignore

I will now give all new writers a piece of advice, both simple and excellent, that most of you will immediately ignore:

Never read reviews of your work.

A negative review, especially of their first published story, can send a beginner into a downward spiral of self-doubt that completely torpedoes their confidence and ability to write new stories. I've seen it happen too many times to good, promising young writers.

But most beginners will ignore the above advice, because new writers crave validation. They lack confidence, so they eagerly and obsessively Google for reviews of their work, hoping to have their fragile egos stroked and to bask in the effusive praise of strangers.

And they will read whatever they find. If it's a bad review, cue the despair and hand wringing. If it's a good review, cue the over-inflated ego. Reviews send beginning writers to one extreme or the other on the Arrogant or the Fearful Beginner spectrum.

Remember, a review, good or bad, is just one person's opinion. One person out of seven billion. It means nothing. Your story has already been published. Someone liked your story so much that they paid you money for it. That is what counts — and the *only* thing that counts.

A Safe Approach to Reviews

Few of you will follow my advice of never reading reviews of your work. Your need for validation is too great. Emotion will override intellect.

And in truth, reviews do provide *one* item of value to a writer: pull quotes. Pull quotes are the extracted positive parts of a review, great for posting on your website, your blog, or on book covers when you get to the point of doing a collection.

So how can you find great pull quotes if you never read reviews of your work?

The safest approach for a beginner is to enlist a trusted friend or family member who is supportive of your writing dream. Ask them to set up a permanent Google alert (www.google.com/alerts) containing your writing name and your story names. Or set up the alert yourself and forward your helper any results it generates. Explain to your helper that their role is to read the reviews and filter out the negative ones, providing you with a list of only "safe" reviews to read.

Seem like a lot of trouble? Think you're tough enough to handle a bad review? Shrug. Your career. Your decision. But you've been warned.

Pull Quotes: The Only Value in Reviews

Pick up any movie section of a newspaper and you'll see pull quotes galore: "This summer's blockbuster," "A must-see thriller," "Action-packed fun," and so on.

Pull quotes are *always* positive. Duh. Hollywood never selects anything negative from a review to highlight. But that doesn't mean the entire review containing a pull quote was glowing. The studio might have extracted "action-packed fun" from a passage that read, "Despite the miscasting of Stallone as the ballet dancer and the wooden acting of the supporting cast, the shoot-out finale at the Bolshoi provides plenty of action-packed fun."

How to Do Pull Quotes

Let's say your review-screening helper has sent you a positive review of your story. You want to grab pull quotes to post in your blog and website. What's the proper approach?

Here are the basic rules for use and formatting of pull quotes:

- Most importantly, whatever you pull out *must remain true to the intent of the reviewer*. If my fictional movie review above had said "Boring throughout, with only the shoot-out at the Bolshoi providing a sadly short-lived bit of action-packed fun," then the pull quote would have been straining the reviewer's intent. Hollywood would still probably use the quote, but you shouldn't as a writer.

- If you have multiple great quotes in a review separated by text you don't want, then use ellipses (...) to indicate where you have deleted text.

- If you drop original text as above, you may need to change or add words to make the quote grammatically correct or to continue to make sense. Any words you add not in the original review should be enclosed in square brackets, [like this].

As an example, consider this fictitious review:

"In her brilliant debut story, Willa Newbie (not to be confused with William Newbee, whose new novel we review tomorrow) introduces us to an ensemble of likeable, believable characters caught in a post-apocalyptic scenario that she brings to an emotionally satisfying resolution."

You might pull the following quotes from the above:

> "[A] brilliant debut story...likeable, believable characters...an emotionally satisfying conclusion."

Or:

> "[A] brilliant debut story...[with] likeable, believable characters...[and] an emotionally satisfying conclusion."

If you want to see examples of pull quotes, check out my review page on my website: www.smithwriter.com/reviews.

One Last Warning

Another critical piece of advice.

If you write, don't review.

I find it head-shaking strange the number of writers, mostly beginners, who write reviews. Dumb, dumb, dumb for so many reasons.

First, it's an astounding waste of time. You're a fiction writer. Your time is precious. So write, but write stories and novels, not reviews.

Next, being a reviewer offers *zero* upside for your writing career. It won't raise your profile as a fiction writer. You want profile? Write more stories and get them published. And you can't do that if you spend valuable writing time doing reviews.

Most importantly, although being a reviewer has no upside, it does have a *major* downside. Unless you write only positive reviews, you are going to make enemies, including the author, acquiring editor, and publisher—people who have a financial stake in that story, publication, or author's career.

And those people will remember you—and not fondly. They'll remember you when *your* stories are published, when you submit stories to their publication, when you are up for awards—whenever they can have any possible impact on your writing career.

Don't think people are that petty? Say, you're new around here, aren't you? Shrug. Your career, your decision.

I also think it's unfair to criticize the work of another writer, no matter how much you disliked it. Remember, this is only your opinion. You are not stating some universal truth. And consider how you would feel if another writer eviscerated your fictional baby (yeah, that metaphor is intentional).

It also makes you look jealous and petty, tearing down a better writer to your level. Don't like what they did with that story? Think you can do better? Prove it—go write a story, not a review.

If you really feel you simply must give your opinion on how that writer could have made that particular work better, send them a personal, non-public note.

If you remain enamored with being a reviewer, consider only reviewing works you truly admired and enjoyed, where you can be positive and help your fellow writers. But my advice remains the same...

If you write, don't review.

If you're interested, here are two posts by social media writer, Kristen Lamb, on the topic of writers as reviewers:

- warriorwriters.wordpress.com/2013/06/20/
  should-authors-write-bad-book-reviews/
- warriorwriters.wordpress.com/2013/06/21/is-it-fair-for-authors-to-review-other-authors-do-we-ruin-the-magic/

CHAPTER 18.

LET THE BAND RING OUT AND THE BANNERS FLY:

Promotion (or Not)

So FAR IN this section, which deals with what happens when you finally sell a story, we've covered short fiction contracts, working with an editor, what your first sale *really* means, and dealing with reviews.

To finish this section, we discuss the issue of promoting your first published story. Later, in Section Five, we'll discuss promotion more broadly, for you as an author and for all your published works. For now, for the situation where you've sold your first story, let's start with a simple question.

How Much Promotion Is Too Much?

And the answer is: most of what you're planning.

Look, I get it. You've sold a story to a well-known professional market. You've dealt with the editing process professionally and graciously. Your story has been published. You've survived your first reviews, which hopefully were glowing (even though they mean nothing).

Good for you. Congratulations again. So now you should promote the hell out of this amazing accomplishment, right?

Wrong.

Why? Because, as I said, you've sold a story. *A* story. One. Singular. Big whoop. Yes, to you as a beginner, it really *is* a big whoop. I remember. But in the world of publishing, you're a newbie. No one cares, aside from you and your mother (and she's just being polite).

Oh, while we're on the topic...this sale you made was to a professional market, right? If not, please immediately cease *any* ideas about promotion. You'll only embarrass yourself.

So What Should You Do?

Well, you could do something like...oh, gee, I don't know, maybe... WRITE? You're a WRITER, remember? Not a PR machine.

Go write your next story. Or two. Or three. Or submit your next batch of stories. Preferably both.

But *please* don't start promoting yourself from the rooftops or their social media equivalent. If you want to build your writing career from the fine start you've just given it, go write more stories and send them out. Rinse and repeat.

> *Visibility through publication is the best promotion for a writer.*

Remember, it's a numbers game—the writers with the most stories in the mail will win.

But Can't I Do Something?

Yeah, okay. I get it. You want to wave your flag a little. No problem. Just don't overdo it. When you learn about the sale, do a tweet, a post to Facebook, and a blog post (and if you don't have a blog yet, don't worry about it for now).

When the story comes out, repeat all of those, including a scan of the cover (hopefully with your name on it) and a link to where your growing legion of fans can buy the magazine or anthology.

Also, don't forget to update your standard cover letter to include your brand-new first professional sale. Read Chapter Eight on cover letters and why you should *not* include non-professional credits.

If your response to any of the above was "but I don't tweet or blog or Facebook," don't worry about it. Go write your next story. And the next. And the next.

Later, in Section Five, we'll discuss a minimal set of "discoverability" tools an *established* writer needs. That's not you (yet). For now, just focus on writing and selling more stories.

Your Career, Your Decision

At this point, as a beginning writer, if you want to know more about promotion, you've entirely missed the point of this short but important chapter.

But, hey, it's your career, your decision. If you want to spend time promoting your single story sale, knock yourself out.

But my advice is to forget about promotion for now. Go write instead.

~~~

This wraps up Section Three on what happens after you sell your first story, from the contract to working with an editor to make that story as good as it can be, to finally seeing it published and reviewed.

Next, in Section Four, we'll look at how your options for marketing and selling your short fiction expand as you sell more stories and begin to build a backlist.

SECTION IV

THE MAGIC BAKERY:

HOW TO LEVERAGE YOUR STORIES

IN THIS SECTION, we'll discuss your options for re-selling your stories after they've been published for the first time. These options include standard reprints, foreign language reprints, audio market sales, and other possibilities for your backlist such as putting out your own collection.

We'll finish up with a discussion of the options independent publishing now presents for the short fiction writer for their backlist. More importantly, we'll look at whether you should consider that route for *first* rights sales.

CHAPTER 19.

HAVING YOUR CAKE
AND EATING IT TOO:

A Writer's Magic Bakery

BEFORE WE START discussing how to resell your short fiction, you need to do some review homework. Please take the time right now to refresh your understanding of two earlier chapters:

- Chapter Three, on understanding the licensing of rights for fiction; and,
- Chapter Fourteen, on contracts, but specifically on protecting the rights to your short fiction and ensuring those rights revert to you.

Stop. Have you reread those chapters? More importantly, do you *understand* those chapters?

Yes, I know—I keep repeating how important those two chapters are. Because they are. If you don't understand licensing rights for your fiction, you're going to get into trouble. Legal trouble. Trouble editors and publishers will remember you for, and not in a good way.

More importantly, if you don't apply the advice on licensing when you start to sell your stories, you will never be able to *resell* those stories—because you will no longer own the rights to them. They won't be *your* stories anymore. They'll belong to whomever you sold the rights.

So seriously, read and reread those chapters now if you haven't already before you dive into this section.

Eating Cake and Licensing Rights

The proverb says "you can't have your cake and eat it, too"—if you eat your dessert, it's gone. You don't get to eat it a second time.

But what if it wasn't gone? What if you could eat it, and then, *abracadabra*, it was still there for you to enjoy again?

Well, for writers, if we think of our fiction as the cakes we bake and of selling them as tasting their yummy goodness (or letting our readers taste them), we can do exactly that. We can sell a story, but still have it available to sell again.

That is, we can *if* we understand the licensing of rights and didn't give away all our rights forever in our first sale of that story.

The Magic Bakery

Writer Dean Wesley Smith calls this a writer's "magic bakery." Your stories and novels are your cakes and pies. When you sell them from your bakery, they magically reappear on your shelves, ready to be sold to the next customer who walks into your store. The time it takes for them to reappear in your bakery is determined by the timing of the reversion clauses in the contracts you sign.

Of equal importance, you don't need to sell the whole cake at once. You can think of licensing rights to your fiction as selling that cake (your story) one slice at a time. See Chapter Three for a full discussion of the possible ways you can slice and sell a short story. Here's a short list:

- First print rights in English;
- First electronic rights in English;
- Second rights in English (reprints, both print or electronic);
- First audio rights in English; and,
- First rights in a foreign language (multiplied by as many languages as you can think of).

To simplify this discussion, I took the geography "slice" (e.g., First North American print rights), which I covered in Chapter Three, out of the above list. These days, most professional markets require First World Rights in English, so geography should not play a part (except for foreign language rights, which we'll discuss later).

A Reminder: The Two Rules for Rights

We covered this in detail in Chapter Fourteen on short fiction contracts, but I'll repeat it here as a reminder. If you want a magic bakery, you need to follow two key rules:

> *Rule #1:* License as few rights to your story as possible when you *first* sell it.

> *Rule #2:* Ensure those rights revert to you after a reasonable time.

Rule #1 means selling as small a "slice" of your story "cake" as you can.

Rule #2 means ensuring you can resell your story again (second rights) as a reprint, or in a collection, or even as a stand-alone ebook. If your contract didn't have a good reversion clause, those rights never come back to you.

Break Rule #1, and you've sold your entire cake for the price of a slice. Break Rule #2, and that cake will no longer magically reappear on your shelves—it's gone forever.

The rest of this section assumes you followed the above rules and your stories have now been published in wonderful professional markets. Also, because you signed good contracts, you still hold all other first rights for those stories, and the first rights you did license have reverted to you so you can sell those stories again.

Let's review how you can leverage those rights and start your own magic bakery.

CHAPTER 20.
THIS STORY FIRST APPEARED IN... :
Selling Reprints

WHAT WE COMMONLY call selling reprints is legally referred to as *licensing second rights*. To simplify it, we'll start with learning how to sell reprints in English and in print (including electronic) only. We'll cover foreign language reprints in the next chapter and other rights later.

Selling a Story Again (and Again, and Again)

A reminder that although we call these "second" rights, you can license second rights a third, fourth, or fifth time. Or more. You can sell a reprint of the same story as many times as you can find a market willing to publish it. I've sold my most published story, "Spirit Dance," a dozen times in English (plus another twenty times in foreign languages) to both print and electronic markets. But no matter how many times you sell a reprint, you are still licensing *second rights* for *each* of those instances.

Finding Markets for Reprints

Selling a reprint involves the same process of finding and submitting to markets for selling first rights to that story (see Section Two). The only difference is that you are now looking for markets that accept reprints.

You find those markets the same way you found first rights markets, by using one of the online market resources we covered in Chapter Six. I again recommend you use www.ralan.com as your primary source.

Ralan identifies whether a market accepts reprints with a simple yes / no flag. Just go to his "Pro Markets" page or his "Anthology" page and do a search for "Reprints: yes." Some markets may say "Reprints: query." Leave these to the end of your list. Selling a reprint to those markets involves more work and a lower probability of success.

Payment for Reprints

You'll likely earn much less for a reprint. A market that pays professional rates for first rights will usually pay at most half of that for a reprint and more likely only 1-2 cents per word. But remember your magic bakery. You've already sold this story to a pro market for good money (or what counts as good money for short fiction). Anything else you make from this story is a bonus. It's found money.

Because of that, when selecting reprint markets, I ignore my most important rule (okay, one of my most important rules) for selecting first rights markets. You don't need to restrict your market search only to markets that pay professional rates. If fact, if you do, you won't sell many reprints.

If you can find a market that pays you pro rates for a reprint, that's great. Just don't expect it. My advice is if you can sell a reprint, then sell it. It's more money for you, it keeps your name out there, and it might garner you new fans who missed the story in its original publication.

The Cover Letter for a Reprint

When selling a reprint of a story, your cover letter *must* inform the editor that the story has been previously published and where it first appeared. I usually modify my cover letter to include this information in the *first* paragraph as follows:

> Dear <editor's name>:
>
> Please find <attached / enclosed / below> my 5,900-word story "State of Disorder" for consideration for <market name>. This story first appeared in the US magazine, *Amazing Stories* (#595) in 1999. It was a finalist for the Aurora Award in 2000.

The balance of the cover letter is identical to what you learned in Chapter Eight.

Note you can also mention if the story's first publication resulted in any awards or "best of" anthology selections. That information is optional, but clearly identifying the reprint status of your story is mandatory.

Simultaneous Submissions for Reprints?

In Chapter Nine, we discussed why you should never "sim-sub" — submit the same first rights story to more than one market at the same time. Reread that chapter now if you need a refresh on why sim-subs are a serious no-no.

But what about simultaneously submitting previously published stories to multiple markets? You can resell these as many times as you're able to find markets willing to publish them, so why not sim-sub?

Well, yes, *legally,* you could resell the same story to multiple markets at the same time. I said legally. I'd still advise against doing sim-subs on reprint stories. The editor will not be thrilled if they buy your reprint story only to discover it in another market at the same time it appears in their magazine or anthology.

So for another reason, this time out of professional courtesy, my advice remains the same:

> *No simultaneous submissions—even for reprints.*

Some Familiar Advice

Once you're familiar with selling the first rights to your stories, selling reprints is an easy extension to what you already know. So have fun and good luck.

My only remaining advice is to repeat what I've said all along for your first rights stories, because it applies to your already-sold stories:

Keep them in the mail.

If your stories can be sold again as reprints, keeping them in your electronic drawer does you no good. Get them out in front of a reprint market.

CHAPTER 21.

BONJOUR / HOLA / CIAO:

Selling Foreign Language Rights

Now THAT YOU understand selling reprints in the English language, let's look at selling to the many non-English language magazines and anthologies published around the world.

Again, you need to ensure you understood these two earlier chapters:

- Chapter Three, on the licensing of rights for fiction; and,

- Chapter Fourteen, on contracts, specifically on protecting the rights to your short fiction and ensuring those rights revert to you.

Why Submit to Foreign Language Markets?

Especially if you can't read that particular language? The reasons are similar to those for selling reprints to English markets.

First, anything you make from these sales is found money. You'll generally get less for foreign reprints than for selling first rights to a professional English market, but you can sell your story in *multiple* languages. My foreign language sales have averaged over $100 per sale, so with sales to several foreign markets, you can easily pick up an additional few hundred dollars per story.

Second, like any sale, it broadens the audience of readers who gain exposure to your work. If you also write novels (or plan to), a resume of short stories in non-English markets can assist in foreign rights sales for your longer work, as can the relationships you'll build with foreign publishers, editors, translators, and illustrators.

Third, there's the fun factor of seeing your byline beside some of the biggest names in fiction. Even when I was starting out, my foreign language sales let my name appear alongside the likes of Stephen King, Neil Gaiman, James Branch Cabell, and H.P. Lovecraft.

Finally, many foreign magazines include beautiful illustrations for your story that you won't get in even pro English markets and that make a great visual addition to your website.

How to Find Foreign Language Markets

Here I'll recommend my own Foreign Market List (FML), which I maintain on my website at http: //smithwriter.com/foreign_market_ list.htm. Here, "foreign" means non-English. The FML lists over seventy active foreign markets in thirty-three languages / countries, organized alphabetically by country.

For each market, I include its website, the name of the acquiring editor, postal and/or email address, and details about the types of stories they publish, including genre, word length, pay rates, and how to submit.

How to Select a Valid Foreign Language Market

Before you run to the FML and start submitting, let's discuss how best to choose a foreign language market. Here are the rules I follow:

> *Rule 1: Never submit a story to a foreign language market until you've first sold it to an English language market.*

Many of the top English genre fiction markets have foreign language editions or will ask for foreign language rights. Selling a story to a non-English market first *could* jeopardize a more prestigious and lucrative English first rights sale. In addition, most foreign language markets prefer if your story has the credentials of a major English market.

Rule 2: You are looking for markets that accept unsolicited submissions.

Although most foreign language magazines publish reprints from English markets, many select those stories themselves by reviewing the top magazines such as *Asimov's* or *The Magazine of F&SF*. They will then approach the author or editor directly to acquire rights. Alternatively, some foreign markets have an agreement with the top English language magazines to reprint selected stories. That is why some top English pro markets purchase foreign language rights, as mentioned above.

Regardless, such markets don't accept direct submissions from an author. You may still end up with a story in these magazines, but you have no control over the decision, beyond writing a great story and selling it to a top English market.

Rule 3: Unless you are multi-lingual, you are looking for markets that accept submissions in English and will translate your story at no cost to you.

In my experience, any market that accepts submissions in English will also translate at no cost. Some markets, however, accept reprints and unsolicited submissions (rules 1 and 2), but only in the language of their magazine.

The above three rules lead us to the following definition:

A *valid foreign language market* is one that accepts unsolicited submissions in English of stories that first appeared in English language markets, and translates them at no cost to the author.

In my Foreign Market List, I identify the valid markets, flagged as paying or non-paying, as follows:

$$$ – Confirmed valid market (paying)

YES – Confirmed valid market (no pay or pays in copies)

The FML also includes "non-valid" markets, with the following flags:

NO – Market exists but does *not* accept unsolicited subs in English

DEAD – Dead market

??? – Market under investigation or questionable

Why do I include non-valid markets if you shouldn't submit to them? I'm just trying to make it easier for you. If I didn't, and you discovered a market not on the FML, you wouldn't know if it's one I've already found and classified as a "No," or a possible new valid market of which I'm not aware.

Submitting to Foreign Language Markets

Follow the same rules as you would if submitting to an English market in a foreign country: proper manuscript format, cover letter / email, SAE and IRC for snail mail submissions. Chapter Eight covers the proper short fiction submission process. Almost all these markets now take submissions by email, but check the market's FML entry for how to attach your story (text in body, type of file attachment, etc.).

And yes, you can submit in English. You don't need to get your cover letter translated. If the magazine accepts submissions in English, the editor can read English.

The Cover Letter for a Foreign Language Submission

Your cover letter for these submissions should follow the same guidelines we reviewed when submitting a reprint to an English market in Chapter Twenty. That is, it should inform the editor the story has been previously published and where it first appeared, in the first paragraph as follows:

Dear <editor's name>:

Please find <attached / enclosed / below> my 5,900-word story "State of Disorder" for consideration for <market name>. This story first appeared in the US magazine, *Amazing Stories* (#595) in 1999. It was a finalist for the Aurora Award in 2000.

However, unlike when you are submitting reprints to English markets, you don't *have* to mention this information. It's optional, but it will help you sell the translated reprint, especially if you sold to a top professional English market.

Simultaneous Submissions for Foreign Language Markets

Here the situation is similar yet different from what we discussed in Chapters Nine and Twenty with English markets. Again, if you understand licensing of rights, the rules you need to follow should be obvious.

As before when selling English rights, never simultaneously submit the same story to more than one market *in the same language*. A French publisher is not going to be happy if they buy your story for translation and find it in another French publication at the same time.

However, note that restriction "in the same language." There is nothing wrong with submitting a story to a French market at the same time you submit it to a German and an Italian market. Why? Because you license different rights to each of those markets. A French market will want First French Language Rights, while a German market will only need First German Language Rights. Those rights don't conflict with each other.

Selling Second Rights to Foreign Language Markets

Again, if you understand the licensing of rights, you'll know how to handle this scenario as well. But let's make sure.

The *first* time you sell a story in a foreign language (regardless of whether you've sold it in English yet), you are licensing *first rights in that language*. First rights, got it? Not second rights, even if you've sold that story already in English. Rights relate to a language.

However, once you've sold your story once in that language, any future time you submit to any market that publishes *in that same language*, you will be offering *second rights in that language*.

If this seems confusing, you don't understand rights and licensing well enough. A way to understand these scenarios is to consider what the same situation would look like if you were dealing with markets in the English language instead of a foreign one. Once you've sold a story in *any* language, you have sold *first rights in that language*, which you can only do once. Any reprint in that same language involves licensing second (not first) rights in that language.

Caveats: Payment

Payment is generally in USD or in Euros for most of the markets on the FML, and many of the paying markets now provide a PayPal option.

However, getting paid can be challenging. Some markets pay only in local currency or via bank transfer, both of which involve banking fees for you. One large market used to require authors to submit an invoice to their payables department before they'd issue a check drawn on a bank in their country. Checks drawn on foreign banks are not easy to cash even in a large North American city. Some markets also deduct a local income tax withholding amount from the payment.

These markets also face the same challenge in staying alive as do English language genre magazines. Many are run on a for-the-love basis, so production schedules can vary wildly, as can the time for receiving your payment and contributor copies.

And these markets can have short lifetimes. I've had about a dozen foreign language sales where the market folded before they could publish my story.

And sometimes, they just don't pay. But that is rare. Out of over eighty foreign language sales, I've had only two situations where I had to involve the SFWA grievance committee to assist me in extracting payment.

Caveats: Response Time

Foreign language markets can take a long time to respond to submissions. But you can submit simultaneously to multiple foreign markets *in different languages* since the rights they purchase are specific to their language. In addition, most respond to email queries regarding the status of your submission.

Caveats: Communication

Communication with the editor of these markets can also sometimes be challenging. Most have excellent written English skills, but some do not. However, in most of the latter cases, the magazine will employ a foreign language acquisition editor, so these difficulties tend to be the exception.

Language can also be a barrier to staying current with these markets. My Foreign Market List includes links to the web sites for most of the magazines, but these sites are generally not in English. Fortunately, I receive regular updates from many of the editors or from submitting authors regarding changes in a foreign language market, and then post these to the FML.

I also provide a list of web-based translation tools on my website at smithwriter.com/translation_sites. These tools can assist you to understand a magazine's website. They can also help on the rare occasion where you receive a reply in the language of the editor.

A word of warning, though. Don't ever use a translation tool to translate from English to the target foreign language and then submit that result, even if it's only your cover letter. These tools simply aren't that good. If you don't believe me, try translating any sentence from English to the foreign language and then back again.

A Story of a Foreign Language Sale

If you're still not convinced of the value of foreign language markets, or if my caveats above have scared you off, let me share one of my experiences. Well, actually, it's a chain of experiences, all resulting from a single foreign language sale.

In 2000, I sold one of my Heroka shapeshifter stories to *Ténèbres*, an excellent dark fantasy magazine in France. The editor, Benoît Domis, asked if I had any more Heroka stories. I sent him the two others I'd written at that point, and he bought both of them as well.

Cool, but there's more. *Solaris*, a long-running and award-winning Québec magazine, also publishes in French but unlike *Ténèbres*, it only accepts stories written in French. It won't translate from English. But I now had a French version of my Heroka stories. Benoît provided the translated versions to me, and I submitted these to *Solaris*, who bought two of them. (By the way, if you sell a translated story, it is standard to split the payment 50/50 with the original translator. You own the rights to your story, but the translator owns the rights to the translation.)

Even cooler, but there's still more. Both stories that appeared in *Solaris* made the final ballot of Canada's Aurora Award for Best Short Fiction in French, and one of them ("Spirit Dance") won the award. As far as I know, I'm still the only person to win the Aurora in both of Canada's official languages.

And there's still more. Benoît told me at the time (2000) that if he ever got his own press, he'd love to put out a collection of my fantasy stories. That was very nice to hear, since I'd just started writing, but I never really expected anything to come of it.

Fast forward to 2010, when Benoît contacted me to say he now had his own small press (Dreampress) and would like to do that collection. Dreampress published *La Danse des Esprits* (*Spirit Dance*) in 2011, and it was a finalist for two French awards, the *Prix Masterton* and the *Prix Bob Morane*.

So five story publications in French, one award win, three award nominations, and my own collection in French—all starting from a single sale to a French magazine.

CHAPTER 22.
CURLING UP WITH A GOOD PODCAST:
Selling Audio Rights

ASIDE FROM SELLING second rights in English or first rights in other languages, you can also resell your story to one of the growing number of podcast magazines. These markets provide a narrator for your story and usually make their audio magazine available online to subscribers as a podcast.

How to Find Audio Markets

As with print and reprint markets, you can find audio markets on Ralan's list at www.ralan.com, on his "Audio" markets page.

How to Submit to Audio Markets

Your cover letter for these markets will be the same as for submitting to a reprint market, which I covered in Chapter Twenty. The key point again is you must inform the editor of where your story was originally published. Audio markets buy First Audio Rights in English (no geography dimension is involved, since they're downloadable).

Submitting to Audio Markets Before Print Markets

You *could* submit to an audio market before you've sold the story to a first rights text market, but most audio markets *prefer* you send them previously published stories. It helps their selection process if a story originally appeared in one of the top pro markets. Therefore, I treat audio magazines as reprint markets.

In addition, selling to an audio market first restricts your choice of print markets to which you can sell first print rights, as many of those print markets will consider your story as having been published if it has appeared in audio form.

CHAPTER 23.
MORE OPTIONS FOR YOUR BACKLIST:

Collections

IN SECTION TWO, we learned how to sell your unpublished stories. This section has focused on reselling those same stories, with the assumption your original contract ensured the necessary rights reverted to you after publication. In both cases and throughout this book, we focused solely on the same types of markets: magazines and anthologies, whether these be print, electronic, or audio.

However, once you've published *enough* short stories, you'll have another option for your backlist (your inventory of previously published stories), namely putting out a *collection*.

A terminology reminder:

> An *anthology* is a book-length work of short fiction by *different* authors.

> A *collection* is a book-length work of stories from a *single* author.

The Best Timing for a Collection

So at what point in your short fiction career should you consider publishing a collection of your stories? The advice has changed considerably in the past decade.

The standard practice used to be for authors to build their name in short fiction, then move on to novels. Once they had established their name in the long form as well, they would publish a collection, often from the same press that published their novels.

But collections never sell as well as novels, so they were always a hard sell with traditional publishers. They became even less popular with publishers when automated inventory systems in the big retail chains started ordering an author's new title based on sales of their previous title. Suddenly those lower sales on collections were depressing pre-orders for the author's next novel. This started a trend for even established authors: to seek out smaller presses to publish their collections.

That shift also prompted a change in when an author should first publish a collection. If an author was going with a small press, they no longer had to publish a few novels before doing a collection.

With no reason to wait, writers began to publish collections as soon as possible. Also, having something published in book-length form gave the writer added credibility and visibility, helping them build a fan base and market a first novel.

So When Is "As Soon as Possible"?

The simple answer is when you have enough strong, previously published stories to fill a book-length volume. That length varies by publisher, but most collections are eighty to a hundred thousand words. Just remember that the longer the book, the higher the costs for the publisher for a print edition.

Some publishers put out much shorter collections. The award-winning UK press, PS Publishing, published my first collection, *Impossibilia*. PS had just started their "Showcase" series, intended to "highlight genre fiction's best up-and-coming writers." Since PS at the time only published print editions and since "up-and-coming writers" would not be widely known, PS reduced their risk by keeping these collections shorter, most being about 30,000 words.

But for planning your collection, aim for eighty to a hundred thousand words.

Putting Together a Collection: Only Your Best

Length is only one factor to consider. You want your collection to be your calling card and something to enhance your reputation as you move to novels. So you'll want to include only your very best published stories, avoiding any weak or even "just okay" tales. The sixteen stories in my second collection, *Chimerascope*, include an award winner, a Best New Horror selection, eight award finalists, and several "Year's Best Fantasy" honorable mentions.

One other consideration: if you plan a novel set in the same universe as one of your short stories, then you want to include that story as well, assuming it's a strong one.

Finally, most publishers will want a *new* story from you, something not previously published. This attracts more buyers, especially your already established fans, since they'll be able to read your new story only if they buy your collection.

Putting Together a Collection: Who's on First?

Once you feel you have enough very strong stories to pitch a collection to a publisher, you'll need to pull them together into a book-length manuscript. Trust me, that is harder than it sounds.

First, deciding on the sequence of the stories in a collection is no simple task. The general wisdom (also followed by anthology publishers) is as follows:

- Start with your best story;
- Place your next two strongest stories in the second and last positions; and,
- Put another strong story in the middle of the book.

The theory is to pull the reader in with a couple of strong entries at the beginning, and finish strong to leave them with a good final memory of the book. Adding another strong tale in the middle as a tent pole prevents the reader's attention from flagging once they get past the opening stories.

Unfortunately, determining your strongest stories is not easy, unless you've been lucky enough to have some award winners or finalists. Remember what we discussed way back in Chapter Five about you being the worst judge of your own work.

But ultimately, different readers have different tastes. I'm often surprised at the stories readers pick as their favorites in my collections.

Personally, I'd recommend you go with the stories *you* are most proud of in the key positions in the collection.

More Sequencing Considerations: Crafting the Reader Experience

A subjective assessment of a story's strength is only one consideration in sequencing your collection. You also must consider the reader's experience as they move from one story to the next. The key considerations include:

- *Length:* Don't put all your longest stories back-to-back. Or your shortest. Mix the lengths of stories as much as possible to give the reader some variety.

- *Genre:* In *Chimerascope,* I wanted to emphasize that I write across multiple genres, so I purposely followed an SF story by a fantasy, then a horror, then a slipstream, etc.. However, you might decide you want to lump all your SF into one section, your fantasy into another. Or even do separate collections by genre.

- *Mood or Tone:* Did you start with a dystopia with a downer ending? You might want to follow that with a story with some hope and promise. Or you might *not* want to place your humorous space opera right after a thought-provoking story so as not to undermine the more serious tale.

- *Stories in a Series:* If you've written multiple stories in the same universe or with the same cast of characters, you'll need to decide whether they appear together or scattered through the book. I had this problem in my translated French collection, *La Danse des Esprits* (Spirit Dances), which included three of my Heroka shapeshifter stories. If you have enough of these stories, you might consider a separate collection just for stories in that world.

Trying to balance these factors (quality, length, genre, mood, series) is a huge challenge since each generally conflicts with at least one other. There's no perfect answer, but if you always keep the reader's experience in mind, you'll come up with a workable order.

Finding a Publisher

As mentioned, collections do not sell as well as novels, so unless you're a Very Big Name (as in Stephen King level), none of the big, traditional publishers will be interested. However, small presses are growing and thriving, and many regularly publish collections.

You need to do your own research to find a small press that's a good fit for your collection, but a good starting point would be to review the recent finalists for Best Collection for the following two awards:

- British Fantasy Award for Best Collection (http://www.britishfantasysociety.org/british-fantasy-awards/the-british-fantasy-awards-a-short-history/)
- World Fantasy Award for Best Collection (en.wikipedia.org/wiki/World_Fantasy_Award_for_Best_Collection).

These are two of the few awards that recognize collections. A review of the finalists for, say, the past three years, will help identify more publishers for your target list, as well as reinforce my point that most collections these days come from smaller presses.

The Indie Option for a Collection

In today's new world of publishing, you also have another option: to publish your collection independently. I'll deal with that in the next chapter when we look at indie publishing for the short fiction writer.

Do Your Research on Publishers

As with any market, you must do your research on any publisher you're considering for your collection. First, confirm they are a fit for your collection by reviewing the types of books they publish.

You also need to look at the business side of working with any prospective publisher. What rights do they ask for? Do they pay an advance? How much? What are their royalty rates? What formats do they produce for their titles? Hardcover? Trade paperback? Ebook?

What distribution agreements do they have in place with the major bricks and mortar bookstores? With the ebook retailers? You want your collection available as widely as possible. If a publisher is weak here, your book will disappear as soon as it is published.

Most importantly, as with short fiction, what does their contract look like? A contract for a collection can be as complex as for a novel. You will want an intellectual property lawyer, preferably one with contract expertise, to review it before signing.

The best research step you can take? For any publisher you are considering, check out their list of authors. Do this for two reasons. First, you should see some names you recognize, names of authors bigger than you. If you don't, this publisher is not likely a good choice for you.

Second, if you can, find a way to contact at least two or three of those authors, especially any at the same point in their careers as you. Ask about their experience with this publisher. Believe me, if they weren't happy, they'll tell you. Writers stick together. I dropped several small presses from my list when I was considering my first collection, based on horror stories from writers who had gone with those publishers.

Another Option: Translated Collections

In Chapter Twenty-One, I dealt with reselling your previously published stories to foreign language markets. Related to this, you also have the option of marketing a collection to a foreign language publisher. However, unless you know some foreign publishers or editors, or unless you're an established name, this will be a harder sell.

One of the advantages I mentioned earlier of selling to foreign language magazines is the relationships you'll develop with those editors and publishers. I also related how selling to the French magazine, *Ténèbres*, led to my French collection, *La Danse des Esprits*, many years later when the *Ténèbres* editor established his own small press.

And as I've said ever so many times throughout this book, the key is to retain the required rights to your stories when you first sell them in English. In this case, you must ensure you don't sell the foreign language rights along with first English rights.

CHAPTER 24.
A BRAVE NEW WORLD:
The Indie Option for Short Fiction

So FAR IN this section, we've covered several ways for you as a short fiction writer to repackage and remarket your backlist of previously published stories, including:

- Selling to print markets that accept reprints (selling second print rights in English);

- Selling to foreign language markets that accept stories that have previously appeared in English markets and will do translations for free (selling first rights in that non-English language);

- Selling to audio and podcast markets (selling first audio rights); and,

- Publishing multiple stories together as a collection to a traditional publisher (including reputable small presses).

In this chapter, we'll conclude the topic of building your magic bakery by dealing with another publishing option: independently publishing your backlist of stories yourself.

We'll also discuss an option I do *not* recommend, that of *originally* publishing your stories yourself.

What Are Your Options?

Writers can now publish their stories as ebooks, either as individual stories or as book-length collections, and to sell them via the major ebook retailers and the writer's website, without needing any third-party publishing intermediary. Writers also have the option of publishing print-on-demand (POD) as well as ebook editions.

The advantages of indie publishing your own work include having full control over how your work is produced, plus a much better royalty rate (more on that later). The disadvantages are the work required (all that control means a lot of decisions to make and tasks to complete) and discoverability of your book (ease of indie publishing means a great deal of competition).

What I Won't Be Telling You

I'm not going to explain the "how" of indie publishing. Why? Well, first, because I'd need another entire book to do that justice. Second, the internet is awash with websites and tools to help with that. Finally, the indie publishing field is changing so fast that whatever I wrote here would be out of date in a month (or less). I will, however, tell you what you will need to do to indie publish.

Indie Publishing Is NOT for First Rights Sales of Short Fiction

Before we go further, let me state my very strong *opinion*: indie publishing is an excellent option for your *backlist*, especially for a collection, but not for *first* rights sales of your stories.

In Chapter Two, I discussed the various benefits of writing and selling short fiction. Go back and read that chapter. If you decide to take the route of indie publishing your *unsold* short fiction, you'll be forsaking most of the benefits of a traditional short fiction career approach.

Building a short fiction career as outlined in this book is fully achievable with work and dedication, and will bring you the full set of rewards outlined in Chapter Two as well as providing you a base to launch a career in novels.

Most importantly, if you publish your short stories yourself, you will have no measure for knowing whether your fiction is any good or whether your writing is improving. If editors of magazines and anthologies keep rejecting your stories, then your writing isn't good enough yet.

Don't think of those editors as gatekeepers, blocking you from reaching readers. Think of them as your coaches, advisors, and protectors. They are helping you become a better writer and protecting you from exposing your work before it has reached a professional level.

So please, don't damage your career by trying short cuts. If you want to be a professional writer, you must become one by learning your craft and your profession. Selling to professional short fiction markets is the surest way of knowing when your writing has reached that level.

Indie Publishing a Collection

But what about when you've sold a bunch of stories to professional markets and you're considering publishing a collection?

Similar to my above position on individual short stories, I still recommend doing collections via traditional publishing, as described in the previous chapter. As explained then, there are significant upsides to doing a collection with traditional publishers, including reputable small presses.

Many writers today would disagree with me, including established pros like Kris Rusch, who wrote the wonderful introduction to this book. Kris and others would recommend the indie route for a collection right out of the gate.

And they may be right. I'm not going to argue strongly one way or the other. Do your research and make up your own mind.

The two routes are not entirely mutually exclusive. If you sign a good contract with a traditional publisher ensuring the rights to the collection revert to you after a reasonable time (say, three years), you can then indie publish a new edition of the collection, either in ebook or POD formats, or both. I did this with both of my English-language collections. *Impossibilia* and *Chimerascope*.

As always—your career, your decision.

Doing It Yourself

If you decide to indie publish a collection, either your own edition after rights revert to you from your original publisher, or a first edition, you'll need to accomplish several things to do it professionally.

First, you'll still need to do everything we discussed in Chapter Twenty-Four about publishing a collection: selecting the stories, deciding on sequence, etc. Go back and read that chapter if you haven't already.

Becoming a Publisher

Next, understand that if you go the indie route, you become a *publisher* as well as a writer—which means becoming conversant with all the challenges and possible approaches that entails. I'd strongly recommend (again) you spend time reading Dean Wesley Smith's "Thinking Like a Publisher" blog series as well as Kristine Kathryn Rusch's "Business Rusch" blog series. Both contain a wealth of excellent and free advice. Just be warned—you have a lot of homework. But it will be worth it.

Do Your Research: The Retailers

Next, research the major ebook retailers and understand their terms of service. The top ones include Amazon (still the 500-pound gorilla), Kobo (my pick for the up-and-coming challenger), Apple (through their iBookstore on iTunes), and Barnes & Noble. Another early contender, Sony, has now sold their ebook business to Kobo. Others include DriveThru Fiction and OmniLit / AllRomance.

In addition, several *aggregator distributors* exist who offer a single route into a variety of the major ebook retailers. Just understand that aggregators take their own royalty cut from each sale. The longest established is Smashwords, but Draft-to-Digital is becoming a popular alternative. XinXii is a European-focused option, as well.

The main advantage of these aggregators is that they provide an easy route into the iBookstore for Apple, into Barnes & Noble for non-US writers like me, and into libraries. You can also pick up sales from the aggregator's own retail channel. OmniLit, although not primarily an aggregator, also offers an option to get into the iStore.

In terms of POD options, the two major ones are CreateSpace (Amazon) and Lightning Source, both of which give indie publishers routes into bricks & mortar bookstores and libraries.

The terms and conditions for working with each of these retailers vary, so you'll need to research each of them separately.

Do Your Research: Pricing

To simplify things for this topic, I'll deal with just the big two ebook retailers. If you're selling ebooks on Amazon and Kobo, you'll earn a 70% royalty on the selling price of an ebook if it's above a certain minimum price (at least $2.99 for Amazon and $1.99 for Kobo), and 35% if it's below that threshold. My numbers assume you're going direct to Kobo rather than through an aggregator. So, for example, an indie-published collection priced at $6.99 will earn the author $4.90 for every copy sold.

Also, Amazon and Kobo allow you to price your book differently in each country in which they distribute. You can let your ebooks default to the equivalent in each country of the US price. But your books will then show very strange prices in those markets, not the preferred X.99 format that helps sell books and looks normal to buyers. Setting individual prices by country for each of your ebooks is preferred, but also more work for you.

POD books bring even more pricing considerations. Print books have a physical production cost, as well as a shipping cost, which drives your minimum selling price. In addition, to get into bricks and mortar bookstores, you must price your book *high* enough to be able to offer bookstores the 40-45% discount they typically expect on orders.

Print Edition or Just Ebook?

Armed with the knowledge from the research you've done on the ebook and POD retailers, you'll now need to handle all the tasks a publisher normally would. One of the first is to decide if you're going to produce your planned collection only in ebook format, or whether you'll also produce a POD edition.

I strongly recommend doing both, and the following discussion assumes that. Print isn't dead and isn't going away anytime soon. You want to reach as many readers as possible, and print readers and ebook readers are two different animals. In addition, having a higher priced print edition helps drive sales of the cheaper ebook edition.

Just understand that putting out a POD edition involves a higher cost and more work than an ebook edition.

Ask a "Name" Author to Write an Introduction

Including "Introduction by <Famous Writer>" on your cover and marketing copy will help sell your book, especially if your stories would appeal to the fans of Famous Writer. A good introduction will also provide a great pull quote for the cover or back cover and on the book's listing on any retailer site.

Don't know any famous writers yet who'd be willing to do this for you? Then you're probably not ready to publish a collection. If you do approach a pro writer to do an introduction, offer to pay them an honorarium. A typical range for such an honorarium is $50-$100.

Hire a Professional Cover Designer

Unless you are a professional graphic designer, do *not* try to do your own cover. Yes, you can find ever so many tools to do this type of work, and yes, ever so many indie writers do their own covers.

Which is why so many indie books have truly horrible covers.

It's not so much the art used that makes these covers awful. It's the design—the choice of fonts, of colors, of placement of title and author name and other text. Plus a dozen other things that need to blend artistically that I can't explain but a professional graphic designer could.

Hire a Professional Editor

Assuming you're publishing a collection of your *backlist* with perhaps one new story, then most of your stories have already appeared in top markets and were professionally edited before publication.

If they weren't, you'll need to hire a line and copy editor. Even if each story did receive a professional edit, you'll still need an edit to ensure consistency of style across the stories, since these likely appeared in different publications. Consistency issues include British versus American spelling, formatting of em-dashes and ellipses, punctuation decisions like the Oxford comma, and many other style issues.

POD and Ebook Design and Production

Designing the interior of a print book is another professional skill you don't have. Trust me, you don't. Hire someone. The same advice holds true for ebook design and creation, although less so. A number of tools exist to help you with ebook formatting and creation. One of the better ones is Jutoh.

By the way, you will want, at a minimum, to make the ebook available in .mobi (Kindle), .epub (every other ereader), and PDF (because some sites still sell a surprising number of PDF copies, especially OmniLit/AllRomance).

Retail Channel Placement

Once you have your book editions ready for sale, you'll need to set up accounts for the various retail channels listed above, learn how each channel works, load your content along with your book's description & keywords, and decide on pricing for each geographic market. More decisions and work for you.

The WIBBOW Test

Does all the above sound like a lot of work? Good, then I've done my job.

Because it *is* a lot of work. I've probably left out several sub-tasks as well. As I said earlier, if you take this route, you are becoming a publisher with all that role entails.

For all of this, as with any writing activity you are considering, you need to ask yourself one key question, which I'm stealing from a writer friend, Scott William Carter, who came up with this: Would I Be Better Off Writing? (WIBBOW).

Because, before anything else, you are a *writer*. Whatever time you spend being a publisher (or even worse, being a promoter) is time you can't be writing new words of fiction. And new words should always be your priority.

You can reduce the work involved in this indie process (and leave more time to be a writer, not a publisher) by using a reputable indie publishing service. I've used Lucky Bat Books for all of my indie publishing projects and would highly recommend them (http://www.luckybatbooks.com/).

An important note: only use a publishing service that charges on a one-time, fee-for-services basis. Never use a company that will take a share of your future royalties. Yes, it will cost you more initially, but you will make it back quickly and be further ahead in the end.

Indie Publishing Individual Stories: Why I Did It

What we've covered in this chapter applies only to your backlist. Yes, you can take this approach for new short stories, but as I explained earlier, I strongly recommend against it.

However, you can indie publish any of your already published stories as *individual* ebooks. You likely wouldn't do POD versions, as they're too small and would be far too expensive to interest any reader.

A couple of years ago, I individually published twenty-four of my previously published short stories as ebooks (which you can check out at www.smithwriter.com/store). My main reason was to dip my toe into the indie waters and learn about this new world of publishing. It also helped me raise my profile with readers who have never encountered my stories, giving them a very cheap way to sample my work.

In addition, these ebooks make excellent giveaways and prizes for contests on my website, for mailing list signups, for thank you gifts, for promotions. For example, I include an excerpt from my novel, *The Wolf at the End of the World*, in the ebook edition of my story "Spirit Dance," the story on which the novel is based.

Indie Publishing Individual Stories: Why It's Probably Not for You

So why don't I recommend this for you, if I've done it? Well, if you look at the list of what you must do to publish an ebook, you'll see it becomes very expensive for a single short story. For example, the cost of a cover for an ebook will be the same regardless of how many pages are inside that book. So your cover cost for publishing twenty-four stories will be twenty-four times the cover cost of a collection of those same stories. Similarly, the cost to format and produce twenty-four separate ebooks is much more than that for a single collection.

I got some great deals from artist and indie publisher friends that made it worthwhile for me to go that route, but most of you won't be that lucky. I recovered my costs quickly from my sales, faster than I expected. You may as well, but just understand the risk.

~~~

This completes Section Four, where we've looked at leveraging the rights you've retained for your short fiction to sell and resell those stories in a variety of ways—in short, to build your own "magic bakery."

Next, in Section Five, we'll take a look at how a short fiction writer's career can progress and how your options expand after you start to sell stories.

SECTION V

IS THAT ALL THERE IS?:

THOUGHTS FOR ESTABLISHED WRITERS

IN THIS, THE final section of our journey, we look at considerations for a short fiction writer once you start to sell often and regularly; that is, once you become established—or at least as established as a short fiction writer can become.

Here, we'll talk about longer term aspects of a short fiction career and paths a writer might choose for their career. Or paths your career might pick all by itself once your credits start to build.

We'll take a look at other pleasant things that can happen as your career matures, such as invitation-only anthologies, awards, and movie options. We'll also review the key discoverability tools for an author, and finish with a discussion of career progression for a short fiction writer.

CHAPTER 25.
COOL STUFF THAT MIGHT HAPPEN:
Awards, Best of Anthologies, Movies

IN THIS CHAPTER, we'll cover the cool things that *might* happen to you after you start publishing stories, or—more likely—a lot of stories. I say *might* because you as a writer have very little control over any of these events—beyond writing the best story you can.

And the Winner Is . . . : Awards for Short Fiction Writers

Once you publish a story, it becomes eligible to be nominated for the many awards given each year for short fiction. Since I'm focusing on speculative fiction genres, I'll restrict my comments to awards for SF, fantasy, and horror. Rather than trying to list all the various awards here, let me point you to a couple of excellent online resources:

- Locus Index to Science Fiction Awards: www.locusmag.com/SFAwards; and,
- Science Fiction Awards Watch: www.sfawardswatch.com/?page_id=3.

I'll also point you to my own "More Links for Writers" page where I list several SF&F award sites: smithwriter.com/more_links_for_writers

Now let's walk through the main types of awards and how an awards process works. What I'm *not* going to do is to tell you how, or encourage you in any way, to promote your freshly minted story for award attention. If you want to know why, then reread Chapter Eighteen on promotion.

A Typical Awards Process

Most awards have a *nomination* phase resulting in a final ballot, followed by a *voting* phase to select the winner(s) from the finalists. Most awards also have multiple categories, such as Best Novel, Best Collection, Best Novella, or Best Short Story.

In the nomination stage, eligible members of a specified group may suggest (nominate) any eligible work in each category for inclusion on the final ballot for the award. At the end of the nomination period, the works (typically limited to five or six) receiving the most nominations in their category are selected for the final award ballot.

Then comes the voting phase, where eligible voters vote by a prescribed method to choose a winner in each category. The voting process can range from simply voting for one work in each category, like on an election ballot, to the Instant Runoff Voting (IRV) method, in which you *rank* multiple selections in each category.

In an IRV ballot approach, the work receiving the fewest #1 votes is dropped in each round and the remaining works proceed to the next round. All ballots that selected the dropped work are now revisited, and the #2 picks for those ballots are added to the vote totals for the remaining works. This continues until only one work remains in each category.

Definition of an "Eligible Work"

What is an "eligible" work? Typically, for a story to be eligible for an award in any year, it must have been published in the *previous calendar year*. Awards are labeled for the year they are *presented*, not for the year the works were published. That is, a 2015 award will be for works published in 2014.

Types of Short Fiction Awards

And what defines an "eligible voter" in the above? Well, it depends on the type of the award. In general, you'll encounter three basic award types:

- Fan-voted;
- Members-only; and,
- Juried awards.

Fan-voted awards allow readers and fans to participate in recommending (nominating) works of short fiction and in voting for who they want to win from among the finalists. The biggest fan-voted awards are the Hugos. Canada's Aurora Awards, Australia's Aurealis Awards, and *Locus Magazine's* Locus Awards are other examples.

Members-only awards restrict eligibility for nominating and voting to members of a particular group. Examples of members-only awards are the Nebulas (restricted to members of SFWA) and the Bram Stoker Awards (restricted to members of the HWA, the Horror Writers Association).

Technically, the Hugos, the Auroras, and many fan-voted awards are members-only awards, since you must be a member of the convention that sponsors and hosts the awards. For example, the Hugos require membership in the previous or current WorldCon (World Science Fiction Convention).

But I still call those awards fan-voted, since anyone can simply buy the necessary convention membership. For the Nebulas and Stokers, you must achieve the required professional publication credits and then apply and be accepted into SFWA or HWA before you are eligible to participate.

Juried awards, our third type of award, use a select group of writing professionals, usually well-known editors, publishers, and writers, to act as a jury. Typically, a separate nominating committee will review eligible works for the year and select a long list for further consideration. The jury may review the long list and make the final short list selection. Or the nominating committee may select the short list, and the jury will only vote on the short list to choose the final winner. Canada's Sunburst Awards and the Endeavor Award in the North-West USA are examples of juried awards.

Writer Awards

There is one other class of awards—those given to writers rather than to specific works.

The John W. Campbell Award for Best New Writer (www.writertopia.com/awards/campbell) is an example of this. Your eligibility for the Campbell begins when you professionally publish a novel with a minimum print run of 10,000, or publish a short story in a professional publication that (a) has a circulation of at least 10,000, or (b) is a SFWA-qualified market, or (c) paid at least three cents per word and fifty dollars for your story.

Your eligibility lasts for two years, and finalists appear on the Hugo ballot, although as I learned when I was a Campbell finalist in 2001, the nice people running the Hugos will tell you over and over (and over) again that the Campbell is *not* a Hugo. However, the Campbell finalists still get one of the cool little Hugo rocket pins, so nyah nyah nyah.

Being Nominated Is Not an Accomplishment

Let me pause to clarify something. Recently, a writer acquaintance declared on their website and Facebook that their novel had been "nominated" for a particular award. Most people interpreted this as meaning the writer's book had made it to the final voting ballot. Much congratulation of said writer ensued, which is natural and good and cool.

One problem. The nomination period for that particular award had not even closed, and therefore the final ballot for the award that year was not yet announced. This writer was crowing that someone had sent in a nomination for the writer's book.

Big whoop. The award in question is fan-voted, so anyone—*including the author*—can submit a nomination. Being nominated is *not* the same as making it to the final ballot. The latter is way cool and is worthy of crowing. The former means absolutely nothing, and if you claim it as an accomplishment, you look naive at best or disingenuous at worst.

The reverse mistake happens, too, where a writer on a final ballot will say they've been nominated for an award. Instead, say you're a *finalist* for the award.

What Awards Mean to a Writer

A boost to your ego—yes. A boost to your sales—not so much. The exceptions are awards that drive purchases by libraries. These tend to be for children's or young adult books, such as the John Newbery Medal (American Library Association) or the Golden Duck Awards (for excellence in children's SF). In the US, many library systems purchase the Newbery winner each year.

But for a short story writer, all an award means is an ego stroke and something to add to your cover letters and website. I've won the Aurora three times and been a finalist for the Campbell, the juried Sunburst, the Canadian Broadcasting Corporation's Bookies, and two juried French awards. I was also a judge for the Endeavors. All were fun happenings and another form of validation, but every time I sit down at my keyboard, I must still write the best story I can. That's all that will ever matter, and that's the way it should be.

A Very Good Year: "Best of" Anthologies

Publication can also mean that your story may be selected to appear in one of the many "best of" anthologies published each year. Again, I won't attempt to list all of these as you can Google them yourself. These contain the "best" stories (in that editor's opinion) published in the prior year. They typically focus on one specific genre, such as the *Year's Best Fantasy* or the *Mammoth Book of Best New Horror*.

These generally are *not* markets to which you submit your published story for consideration. In most cases, the editor(s) make their own selections based on a review of the prior year's issues from the major magazines and anthologies from the big presses. Some editors may invite submissions, but only to find stories they missed, such as those appearing in lesser known magazines or in anthologies from small presses. Even then, the editor typically expects the publisher to submit, not individual authors.

Some "best of" anthologies also include a list of honorable mentions in an index at the back. These are stories the editor enjoyed but ended up not selecting—the writerly equivalent of kissing your sibling.

Lights, Camera, Action

Aside from awards and "best of" anthologies, your published tale could inspire other creative people, resulting in invitations to collaborate on projects based on your story—movies, graphic novels, whatever. I'll give one example from my own experience.

After my story "By Her Hand, She Draws You Down" appeared in *The Mammoth Book of Best New Horror #13*, I began receiving queries about whether the film rights were available. No, not Steven Spielberg or anyone of Hollywood ilk. Most were film students. But one was from Anthony Sumner, who had his own film production company (TinyCore Pictures). Anthony's credits included corporate promotion videos, music videos, and political campaign videos for big name clients—and some short horror movies.

Anthony and I started talking, and the result was a beautiful thirty minute film that screened at film festivals around the world, winning multiple awards. You can read more on that experience and on the film here on my website: www.smithwriter.com/by_her_hand_movie.

You May Now Ignore Everything Above

Awards, "best of" anthologies, graphic novel collaborations, movie deals—possible cool events your story publication may prompt. And they all have one thing in common: you have little or no control or influence over making any of them happen.

So don't sweat trying to make them happen. If they do, they do. If they don't, you're in good company. Always remember: your wisest strategy is to write the best stories you can, submit them to top pro markets, and keep them in front of those markets until they sell. The more stories the better.

CHAPTER 26.
BANDS AND BANNERS REVISITED:
Promotion for Established Authors

IN THIS CHAPTER, we deal with self-promotion for the established writer, both for you and your writing in general.

Once Again: How Much Is Too Much?

The short answer to that question, as in Chapter Eighteen when you'd sold just one story, is again: most of what you're planning.

If you honestly apply the WIBBOW test, you will generally be further ahead if you forget your promotion ideas and instead sit down and write your next story. Or two. Or three. Or get your next batch of submissions out there. Preferably both.

Go write more stories and send them out. Rinse and repeat. Visibility through more sales is always the best promotion for a writer. Remember, it's a numbers game. Most stories in the mail will win.

Discoverability Tools for a Writer: The Minimalist's List

However, yes, there are a minimal set of discoverability tools any established writer needs. Note that I call these *discoverability*, not promotion, tools. Whatever you do related to "promotion" should focus on making you and your fiction discoverable by readers and to help readers connect with both you and your work. These tools will help with those goals.

Here's my list, in priority order:

- *Web Site*: Here's my site: smithwriter.com. Take a tour, and also check other writers' sites. As a beginner, you won't need all the pages I have. However, you'll want what I list under "About Me": your writing bio, a photo (of you, not your cat), your soon-to-be-growing list of published fiction, a review page for your pull quotes, a contact page, and a way to subscribe to your mailing list (more on mailing lists below).

- *Blog:* My site has an integrated blog (smithwriter.com/blogs/douglas_smith) because that's my preference. Or you could select one of the popular free ones like WordPress. Just make sure you link your blog and website to each other.

- *Twitter Account:* If you've been using Twitter for your non-writing persona, you'll need to get another account for your writing life. Here's my Twitter page: twitter.com/smithwritr.

- *Facebook Account:* For now, just a normal account is fine. You don't need an author FB page yet. Hold off on that until you have a lot more credits and a fan following. This will also force you to still communicate like a friend and human being about non-writing stuff, and keep your "me, me, me" writing posts to FB to a minimum.

- *Mailing List:* You'll build this slowly, as your fan base grows beyond your family and cat. To start, make sure your website allows people to register for your mailing list. Check out my mailing list sign-up page on my website. I use Mail Chimp (mailchimp.com) which I find to be excellent. They offer a free account option that handles up to 2,000 subscribers.

More Advanced Tools

As you grow your writing credentials and start publishing in book format (i.e., not just short stories in magazine and anthologies), or when you start putting up your own backlist as ebooks or print-on-demand books (see Chapter Twenty-Four), you might then consider adding the following:

- *Retailer Author Pages:* Retailer sites like Amazon offer the option of having your own author pages, where readers can easily find all of your books in one spot. Here's my Amazon author page: www.amazon.com/gp/entity/Douglas-Smith/ B0037JUXGM. As you see on the right, it allows me to automatically integrate my tweets and blog posts.

- *Goodreads Author Page:* Goodreads is the leading social media site for readers and reading. Again, once you have book-length works available, you can consider setting up an author page. Here's mine: www.goodreads.com/author/ show/3255974.Douglas_Smith

- *Facebook Author Page:* I don't have one yet. Maybe I'll set one up sometime. Right now, I'd rather be writing.

- *LinkedIn Account and a Google+ author page:* I make more use of my writing life LinkedIn account than my Google+ page, simply because it's easy to automate feeds to LinkedIn from my blog and from Twitter. I haven't found an easy way to do that for Google+. Which brings me to the next topic...

Making It Easy

If you do it right, you can minimize the work needed to ensure your blog posts and tweets gets full exposure across all of your channels.

- Ensure your blog has an RMS feed to which people can subscribe. This feed is also required to automatically imbed your blog posts in other sites. My blog automatically posts to my Facebook and LinkedIn accounts, as well as to my Goodreads and Amazon author pages.

- I also use a free service called Twitterfeed (twitterfeed.com/) to automatically send tweets whenever I make a new blog post, with a link in the tweet to the post.

- You can also set your Twitter account to automatically post to Facebook. This is only advisable if you always want to post the same type of updates to both accounts.

If You Want to Know More, You're Missing the Point

I'm not going to tell you how to use any of the above. The internet is awash with social media "experts" spouting advice on how to write blog posts, how often to tweet, how to pick hashtags, what time of day to post and tweet, etc. ad nauseam.

If you want to chase down any of those experts, feel free. Your career, your decision.

But if you do, as I said in Chapter Eighteen, you entirely missed the point. My advice:

Forget promotion. Go write instead.

CHAPTER 27.
WHERE DO WE GO FROM HERE?:
Career Progression in Short Fiction

IN OUR FINAL chapter before we part ways, we'll look at a typical career progression for a short fiction writer, including events and opportunities that may come your way once you start to sell often and regularly.

We'll also consider long term aspects of a short fiction career and ways to continue to leverage short fiction no matter which path you choose for your career.

Keep Writing, Keep Learning

As I warned in Chapter Sixteen, making your first professional sale does not improve your probability of making your next one. Now and throughout your writing career, you will always face the same challenge: to write the best stories you can and to keep them in front of professional markets until they sell.

If you keep showing up at the keyboard, writing new stories, and learning your craft, your stories will continue to improve. You will become a better writer. You will develop your craft—the craft of your chosen profession. And as long as you keep submitting your stories, they will sell. Remember—it's a numbers game.

So get used to it. Write and submit. Rinse and repeat. At its core, that is the key to having a successful writing career. Write and submit.

And never give up.

Invitation-Only Anthologies

As a short fiction writer's career progresses and their name begins to become known, you may start to receive invitations to "closed" anthologies. These are projects where the editor selects which writers get to submit a story, unlike open anthologies where anyone can throw a story over the electronic transom onto the slush pile.

From an editor's perspective, assuming they know enough professional writers, this approach eliminates that slush pile, greatly reducing their work to select stories for the anthology. They can also be confident they're going to get quality submissions. The downside is they miss a chance to "discover" a new talent, to be the first to publish a future star. But for anyone who has read slush, you'll understand why many editors happily accept that downside.

If you start to develop a name in short fiction, or if a particular editor comes to like your work and style, you may experience the happy surprise of being invited to contribute to such an anthology.

Cool. But understand an invitation does not equate to acceptance. You must still write the very best story you can.

Three other key points. First, most invitation-only anthologies are pre-sold to a publisher. This is a very good thing. It means the anthology is going to be published and you'll be paid. But publishers have schedules, and the editor must deliver this anthology by a specific date. The editor works back from that date to determine when they need stories submitted. This means you *must* not miss that submission date.

Second, most anthologies are built around a theme. Your story *must* hit that theme. You cannot leave the editor scratching their head trying to figure out just how your tale fits to the theme they've already sold to the publisher.

Finally, the editor will have sold the anthology based on a promised word length. The editor uses that total to determine approximately how many stories they need and how long roughly each story should be. If they ask for a 6,000-word story, you'll be okay in the 5,000 to 7,000 word range, but do *not* try to submit a 3,000 or 10,000 word story.

So in summary. Invitation-only anthologies: very cool and a sign you're getting noticed. Critical to success: Write the best story you can—submit on time—hit the word length—hit the theme. Do all of those and you'll have a sale and will confirm the editor's faith in you. Miss badly on *any* of those, and not only will you not sell the story, this editor won't invite you back for any future anthology.

Building Your Toolbox

We discussed in Chapter Two the value of writing short fiction in continuing to learn and practice your craft. Every time I write a short story, I try to do something different—in genre, structure, point of view, characterization, voice, or something else.

In short, I'm trying to add to my tool box and to become more proficient in using the tools I already have. Short fiction is ideal for developing your craft. I can experiment with far more tools over the course of 100,000 words of short fiction in fifteen to twenty-five short stories than I could in a single 100,000-word novel.

So even if you do plan to move to novel length works, my advice is to keep writing short fiction as well. Not for the money (I hope you've figured that out by now), but to continue to improve your craft.

Plotting a Career Path

So what do you want to be when you grow up? I mean, as a writer? Way back in Chapter One, when we began this journey, I asked you to think about that. You should by now have a better answer to that question than you did at that point.

Maybe you've decided this is too much work and time, and you'll give up the idea of being a writer. Or you've sold a story and discovered that's all you wanted, to prove to yourself or to others you could do it. Perhaps you know, although you'll always want to write, short fiction is all you're interested in. Or you want to start writing novels, either now or at a point in the future.

There's no right answer to the question. It's all about what you want—what you feel is right for you. Your dream belongs to you, not to me or anyone else. So what I discuss here is just to make you aware of options to leverage your short fiction in a writing career, no matter what direction you might take that career.

Making Your Short Fiction Work for You

Assuming you want a writing career, either in short or novel length fiction (or both), let's talk about how you can leverage your short stories to help further that goal.

One way is to write a *series* of stories—stories linked to each other in some way. This might be the same universe, same characters, sequential in time—or linked in any other way. This way, if your story universe or main character becomes popular, you have a higher probability of selling other stories in that universe or about that character.

Short genre fiction contains so many examples that I'll name just some of my personal favorites: Fritz Leiber's series of sword-and-sorcery stories around his heroes, Fafhrd and the Gray Mouser; John Brunner's tales about his unnamed and mysterious "Traveler in Black;" and Canadian writer Tanya Huff's high fantasy stories around her wizard heroine, Magdalene. I've done this myself in stories about my shapeshifting species, the Heroka ("Spirit Dance," "A Bird in the Hand," and "Dream Flight").

Those are all examples of writing stories about the same world and characters. There are other ways to write a series. I'm writing a group of stories all inspired by Bruce Springsteen songs and plan to market those as a single collection once I have enough.

Short fiction is also a great way to explore a universe or idea or characters you plan to write about at novel length. Or after you write a short story, you may find it keeps calling to you to explore that world in more detail, leading to a novel you hadn't planned on writing.

Or maybe you have a novel planned already. I wrote my novelette "Memories of the Dead Man" to explore the title character, an enigmatic hero in a post-apocalyptic Earth, from the point of view of other characters in that world, in advance of a novel I plan around the Dead Man. I have two other stories that also explore the universe of that planned novel ("Scream Angel" and "Enlightenment"). It's a way of taking your novel out for a short test drive, to explore ideas and characters.

And if you do eventually write a novel around a story or series of short stories, you will have a built-in audience. You'll also have a great way to drive interest in the novel by re-releasing your short stories in that world, as a collection or stand-alone ebooks or even putting them up on your website.

CHAPTER 28.
SO LONG AND THANKS FOR ALL THE FISH:
Parting Thoughts

THANK YOU FOR taking this journey with me. I sincerely hope you found this book of use and will continue to find it helpful in your short fiction career. I hope you *are* planning a short fiction career and can now begin to see how to best make that dream a reality.

If you're a beginner, each time you finish a story, cycle back through Section Two of this book to ensure you're following all the steps, avoiding any beginner mistakes, and leveraging all the advice on how to submit your stories.

When you sell a story for the first few times, review Section Three to ensure you're signing a reasonable contract and to refresh yourself with how to work with an editor. When you've built a backlist, reread Section Four to help you start your magic bakery.

Once you become an old hand at the process, you can use this book as a reference source on specific subjects such as contracts or licensing of rights.

Please feel free to reach out to me with any questions, thoughts, or suggestions regarding this book. I can be reached at doug@smithwriter.com or via the contact page on my website at www.smithwriter.com/contact. I also invite you to subscribe to my newsletter at www.smithwriter.com/mailing_list.

My sincere best wishes to you for all the success in your writing career.

Whatever you do…

Keep writing.

Start at the top.

Keep it in the mail.

Guard your rights.

Keep dreaming.

Yours in creativity,

Douglas Smith

ABOUT THE AUTHOR

"DOUG SMITH IS, quite simply, the finest short story writer Canada has ever produced in the science fiction and fantasy genres, and he's also the most prolific. His stories are a treasure trove of riches that will touch your heart while making you think."
— *Robert J. Sawyer, Hugo and Nebula Award-winning author*

Douglas Smith is an award-winning Canadian author whose work has been published in thirty countries and twenty-five languages. His recent urban fantasy novel, *The Wolf at the End of the World*, was described in *Publishers Weekly* as "an immersive and enjoyable reading experience. Readers will delight in learning more about Native American mythology, which is skillfully woven throughout the story. Smith's novel is both well paced and deftly plotted."

His short story collections include *Chimerascope* and *Impossibilia*, as well as the translated collection, *La Danse des Esprits*. Doug is a three-time winner of Canada's Aurora Award, and has been a finalist for the John W. Campbell Award, CBC's Bookies Award, Canada's juried Sunburst Award, and France's juried Prix Masterton and Prix Bob Morane.

His website is smithwriter.com, and he tweets at twitter.com/smithwritr. You can sign up for Doug's newsletter at smithwriter.com/mailing_list.

OTHER WORKS BY DOUGLAS SMITH

Novels

The Wolf at the End of the World (Lucky Bat Books, 2013)

Collections

Chimerascope (ChiZine Publications, Canada, 2010) *Finalist for the Sunburst Award, Aurora Award, and CBC's Bookies Award*

Impossibilia (PS Publishing, UK, 2008) *Aurora Award Finalist*

La Danse des Esprits (Dreampress, France, 2011, translated) *Finalist for the Prix Masterton and Prix Bob Morane*

Short Stories

"Spirit Dance" (1997) *Aurora Award Finalist*

"New Year's Eve" (1998) *Aurora Award Finalist*

"State of Disorder" (1999) *Aurora Award Finalist*

"Symphony" (1999) *Aurora Award Finalist*

"What's in a Name?" (2000)

"The Boys Are Back in Town" (2000)

"La Danse des Esprits" (2001) *AURORA AWARD WINNER (French translation)*

"The Red Bird" (2001) *Aurora Award Finalist*

"By Her Hand, She Draws You Down" (2001) *Aurora Award Finalist; Best New Horror selection*

"Scream Angel" (2003) *AURORA AWARD WINNER*

"Jigsaw" (2004) *Aurora Award Finalist*

"Enlightenment" (2004) *Aurora Award Finalist*

"Going Harvey in the Big House" (2005) *Aurora Award Finalist*

"Memories of the Dead Man" (2006)

"The Last Ride" (2006)

"A Taste Sweet and Salty" (2006)

"Murphy's Law" (2006)

"The Dancer at the Red Door" (2007) *Aurora Award Finalist*

"Out of the Light" (2007)

"Bouquet of Flowers in a Vase, by van Gogh" (2008) *Aurora Award Finalist*

"Going Down to Lucky Town" (2008)

"Doorways" (2008)

"Radio Nowhere" (2009) *Aurora Award Finalist*

"Nothing" (2010)

"A Bird in the Hand" (2010)

"The Walker of the Shifting Borderland" (2012) *AURORA AWARD WINNER*

"Fiddleheads" (2013)

"Dream Flight" (2014)

Specialty Books

"By Her Hand, She Draws You Down": The Official Movie Companion Book (2010)

A complete list of Doug's published fiction is available on his website at smithwriter.com along with excerpts and reviews of his work. An excerpt of *The Wolf at the End of the World* is also included in the following pages. All of Doug's works are available as ebooks in a variety of formats.

Join Doug's mailing list at smithwriter.com/mailing_list to be notified of new books and stories, award news, and events Doug will be attending.

CHIMERASCOPE

Chimerascope [ki-meer-uh-skohp]—a story of many parts...

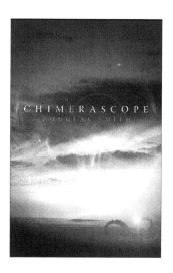

Doug's second collection contains sixteen of his best stories, including an award winner, a Best New Horror selection, and eight award finalists. Stories of fantasy and science fiction that take you from love in fourteenth-century Japan to humanity's last stand, from virtual reality to the end of reality, from alien drug addictions to a dinner where a man loses everything.

"His stories are a treasure trove of riches that will touch your heart while making you think." *—Robert J. Sawyer, Hugo Award-winning author*

"A massively enjoyable trek...all filtered through Smith's remarkable imagination and prodigious talent." *—Quill and Quire (starred review)*

"The 16 stories in this collection showcase the inventive mind and immense storytelling talent of one of Canada's most original writers of speculative fiction." *—Library Journal*

"An entertaining selection of stories that deftly span multiple genres." *—Publishers Weekly*

"An engaging and entertaining volume, pieces of whose content resonate after the book is finished." *—Booklist*

"Douglas Smith is an extraordinary author whom every lover of quality speculative fiction should read. Rating: A+" *—Fantasy Book Critic*

"Arrestingly inventive premises in a field where really interesting new ideas are harder and harder to find. ...Smith is definitely an author who deserves to be more widely read." —*Strange Horizons*

"A beautifully diverse selection of short tales...well-crafted, easily digestible; several of the stories are incredibly moving and stick with the reader long after." —*Sunburst Award jury*

"Smith is a master of beginnings...some of the most well-crafted hooks you'll find anywhere...[with] endings that feel satisfying and right." —*Canadian Science Fiction Review*

For more, please see smithwriter.com/chimerascope.

IMPOSSIBILIA

Aurora Award Finalist

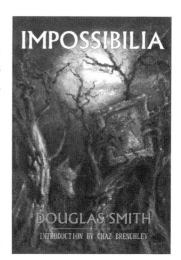

Doug's first collection contains three novelettes, including an award winner and an award finalist. Stories of wonder with characters that you won't forget. Characters who, like any of us, have things they hide inside—secrets, fears, aspects of themselves they keep locked away. Or try to.

Only their things are a little...different.

A painter who talks to Vincent van Gogh

A shapeshifter hunting one of his own

The secret to being the luckiest man alive

Welcome to *Impossibilia*!

"The finest short story writer Canada has ever produced in the science fiction and fantasy genres." —*Robert J. Sawyer, Hugo and Nebula Award-winning author*

"One of Canada's most original writers of speculative fiction." —*Library Journal*

"A great storyteller with a gifted and individual voice." —*Charles de Lint, World Fantasy Award-winning author*

"In the grand manner that harks back to Bradbury and Sturgeon and Ellison." —*Chaz Brenchley*

"In my search for the perfect short story, the three in this volume certainly qualify." —*SF Crowsnest Book Reviews*

For more, please see smithwriter.com/impossibilia.

THE WOLF AT THE END OF THE WORLD

© Douglas Smith *[Novel excerpt]*

Introduction by World Fantasy Award winner, Charles de Lint

The Wolf at the End of the World *takes place five years after the events in Doug's award-winning novelette, "Spirit Dance" (available in his earlier collection, Impossibilia, or as a stand-alone ebook). In the novel, Gwyn Blaidd, the hero of "Spirit Dance," battles ancient native spirits, the shadowy Tainchel, and his own dark past in a race to solve a murder that might mean the end of the world.*

Chapter 1: Mary

Everything had gone wrong, and now Mary Two Rivers was running away. Away from the dam site, away from the damage they'd done, stumbling through the bush in the dark, trying to keep up with Jimmy White Creek and ahead of the security guards. And the dogs. She could hear dogs barking now.

What had she been thinking? Why had she gone along with Jimmy and the rest of them? She was an A student. She was going to university in the fall. She had plans, plans to get off the Rez. Plans that didn't include jail.

Hanging a banner over the dam to protest the loss of Ojibwe land was one thing, but then somebody had poured gasoline on one of the construction vehicles and lit it on fire. And she'd let herself be part of it.

Just because Jimmy had a cute smile and cuter butt—a butt that was getting farther and farther ahead of her as she struggled to keep up. She was a bookworm, not an athlete, and the ground was starting to rise. Jimmy was heading for the west ridge overlooking the still dormant dam and its reservoir lake. She didn't know where the other kids were. Everyone had scattered when the guards appeared, and she'd followed Jimmy. Or tried to.

"Jimmy!" she cried in a desperate whisper. "Wait up!" She didn't know these woods anymore. If she lost him, she doubted she'd get far before the guards caught her.

Jimmy stopped on the hill ahead of her, chest heaving, breath hanging misty in the chill October air. The moonlight caught his pale, sweating face, and in that moment, she wondered how she'd ever thought he was handsome. "Mary, you gotta keep up," he panted, his voice breaking.

"There's a path through the trees on top of the ridge. We'll lose them in there and cut back to the Rez." He started up the slope again, not waiting for her.

Forcing her trembling legs to move, she kept climbing. Jimmy disappeared over the top. Half a minute later, she scrambled up the last few yards. She looked around. Jimmy was nowhere in sight.

The tall jack pines stood closer here, the undergrowth thick between them, their high tops touching, blocking off the cold light from the waxing half moon. Whatever path Jimmy had taken was invisible, hidden by darkness.

She was alone and lost.

She sank to the ground, shaking. She was going to be caught. She was going to jail. What would her parents say? Their dream was for her to get a degree, to beat the odds of being born on the Rez. Their dream....

She swore softly to herself. *Her* dream, too. She stood up, anger conquering her fear. They would *not* catch her. Sucking in a deep breath, she let it out slowly to calm herself as she looked back down the hill she'd just climbed.

The dam and its dark captured lake lay in the distance below. Five burly figures were climbing the bottom of the hill. But worse, ahead of the guards, two gray shadows leapt over the rocks and brush of the slope. The dogs would reach her in less than a minute.

Turning back to the forest, she listened for any sound of Jimmy running ahead. *There.* Had that been a branch snapping deep in the woods? She moved in the direction of the noise, tripping over unseen rocks and roots. One patch of darkness loomed blacker than the rest. She stepped closer. It seemed to be an opening through the trees. Praying for this to be the path that Jimmy had taken, she plunged ahead.

As she moved into the forest, her eyes slowly adjusted to the deeper darkness under the trees, aided by the occasional sliver of moonlight slicing through the canopy of branches above. This was definitely a path. She paused a moment, straining to hear any sound of pursuit. The dogs were still barking, but they didn't sound any closer.

The barking stopped. In the sudden silence, she heard the yip of a fox. She shuddered, remembering a saying of her *misoomish*, her grandfather. "Bad luck," he'd told her as a child. "You hear a fox bark in the night, that's bad luck." But then the dogs took up their call again, and she allowed herself a small thrill of hope. The barking was fainter now. The dogs, and presumably the men with them, were moving away from her. They hadn't found this path.

She was going to get away. The tension gripping her vanished, and her shaking legs gave way. She collapsed onto the soft cushion of pine needles that covered the ground, sweat soaking her t-shirt under her parka. She hugged her knees to her chest, shivering from the chill and the adrenaline still in her.

Now that the immediate danger was gone, another thought came to her. Just last week, a worker had died at the dam site. Animal attack, the cops had said. She swallowed. Because his body had been partially eaten.

Suddenly, huddled on the forest floor in the dark, she didn't feel quite as safe as she had a moment before. She wanted nothing more than to be home in her own bed, to hear her parents in the next room, talking or arguing, she didn't care which, just so long as she was out of this nightmare. With that image filling her heart, she stood and started along the path once more, still praying to catch Jimmy, to have him lead her out of these woods, to lead her home.

A brightness grew ahead. A few seconds later, she stepped into a clearing lit in cold luminescence by the half moon above and enclosed by high rock walls ahead and to her left. To her right, the clearing gave way to the pines again, the level ground sloping away sharply. She walked to the top of the slope, looking for a way down. Her heart fell.

Halfway down, the pines thinned and then disappeared completely where the forest had been cleared near the bottom. The slope ended at the road leading onto the top of the dam. Beyond the dam, the black surface of the lake rippled like some great beast shuddering itself awake in the night.

She'd run the wrong way, back toward the dam.

With a sudden sick feeling, she realized what she should have figured out earlier. The dogs would have followed a scent. They hadn't followed her, so they must have been on Jimmy's trail, which meant Jimmy had taken another path, not the one that had led her here.

She'd taken the wrong path.

She looked around the clearing, searching for some alternative to retracing her steps. The slope below led right back to the dam and the scene of the crime, so that route was out. The dark lake caught her attention again, recalling childhood memories of her grandfather's stories, the ones about the evil spirits that lived in deep water.

She turned her back on the lake and those memories. Enough. Time to go home. She considered the rock walls rising above her. The one facing the entrance to the path was almost sheer and rose too high for her even to think of trying to scale it. The wall facing the lake was less steep and offered some handholds for climbing.

It looked about twenty feet high. She examined its face for the best route, finally selecting a path that would bring her up beside a large boulder perched by itself at the top of the wall.

Or maybe it was a bush, since she saw something move on it, like branches shifting in the wind. Just then, a cloud scuttled across the night sky, swallowing the moon. As the clearing fell dark, she shivered at a sudden strange thought—that the shape had resembled something crouched there, and what she'd seen moving were actually long locks of hair.

Another gust brought a smell down to her, thick and heavy—the smell of mushrooms and rotting wood and wet moss. Bitter, and yet, at the same time, so sickly sweet she thought she would retch.

The cloud hiding the moon moved on. Pale moonlight shone down again, cold and cruel, and Mary finally saw what crouched above her, waiting.

…

[end of excerpt]

Look for *The Wolf at the End of the World* at all major book retailers!

INDEX

.

45388598R00129

Made in the USA
Charleston, SC
18 August 2015